Ooey Gooey Chemistry

Curriculum for Homeschool and Co-op Students

By Marie Ecker

Easy Peasy Science Lab Curriculum

Printed in the United States of America

First Printing, 2017

Edited by Mike Ecker
Cover Illustration: Pigknit

Easy Peasy Science Fair
Satellite Beach, FL 32937

www.EasyPeasyScienceFair.com

Easy Peasy Science Labs
5th – 8th Grade Science Curriculum

Elephant
Toothpaste

Science lessons can be fun for your child and easy on you! This project based unit includes fun labs, interesting assignments, projects and guides for internet resources. Your child will enjoy science as they learn actively.

Check out the awesome labs, demos and activities included in this book!

- Shrinking Marshmallows
- Magic Burning Dollar Bill
- Melting Styrofoam Chemistry
- Oobleck Physical Properties
- Exploding Soap
- Elephant Toothpaste
- Rainbow Flames
- Mentos and Coke Scientific Method
- Acid Attack
- Burning Steel Wool
- Periodic Table Battleship

Easypeasysciencefair.com

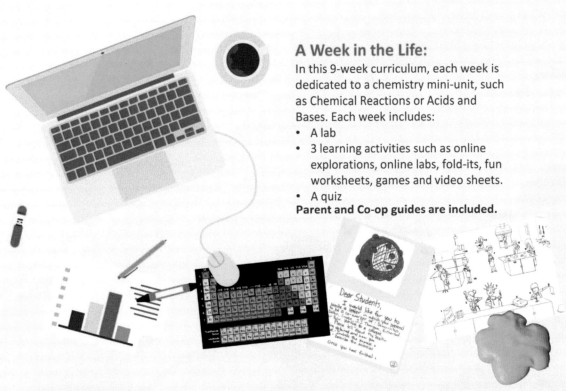

A Week in the Life:

In this 9-week curriculum, each week is dedicated to a chemistry mini-unit, such as Chemical Reactions or Acids and Bases. Each week includes:

- A lab
- 3 learning activities such as online explorations, online labs, fold-its, fun worksheets, games and video sheets.
- A quiz

Parent and Co-op guides are included.

Learning is embedded into our curriculum activities. We believe that the way to engage children is to have them actively participating in their own learning instead of passively reading a textbook. In this book, learning and doing go hand in hand.

Teacher's Guide and Student Workbook

Traditional   Home Friendly

Traditional textbook labs are designed to be done in the science laboratory. It can be expensive and intimidating to replicate them at home or in a co-op. We have adapted our labs so that they can be done as simply as possible at home.

Something as simple as a clothespin on a kitchen pot can replace an elaborate ring stand set up.

Table of Contents

Pacing and Sequence Guides:

In this nine unit Chemistry book, each unit builds upon the other and should be completed in order. Each unit is designed to be a week long. Every unit will have one introductory lesson, one lab, two further explorations and a quiz or culminating project. Each unit teacher's guide provides a suggested sequence and pace. We suggest always completing the introductory (first) lesson of each unit on the first day of that unit. This introductory lesson gives students a good foundation for the rest of the week. Lab days can be moved to the most convenient day for you, and the other weekly lessons can be moved around easily. We recommend finishing a unit before moving on to the next.

We believe in active learning and our worksheets guide students through each lesson activity. Most 5th -8th grade students can work though these lessons independently using their guided lesson worksheet. Each lesson should take about 45 minutes to complete. If 45 minutes is more than your allowed time consider having students complete only half of the assignment each day. This will work for all assignments. For labs, students can complete the lab one day and then do the write-up and answer lab questions on the next day. You could also consider having students complete one assignment every other day.

Labs

We work hard to find educational science labs that are interesting for students to do but can easily be done at home or in a non-lab environment. Our labs use materials that can be purchased in stores you would normally shop in. We want our labs to be easy and accessible. We use convenient household measurements such as cups, teaspoons and tablespoons. We assume that measuring spoons and cups are what many households will use for their science experiments. This is also helpful for Co-ops, smaller schools and elementary level teachers who might not have access to expensive science equipment.

Preparation for labs: Go through the materials list to make sure you have everything needed for the chemistry labs in this book. We find that having the materials on hand means you will be much more likely to do the labs. Your children will thank you for it!

Internet Resource Page

The internet has a vast wealth of resources which are free and interesting to students. We use these resources quite a bit, allowing students to do virtual labs, watch great videos, read non-fiction articles and create their own products. Students will need to have access to the internet to complete many of their lessons. If you do not have a computer for each student you can project a lesson from the computer and all do it together. Finding these resources is time consuming, so we have done the work for you finding what we believe to be the best and most interesting resources for learning. This book includes guides, questions and diagrams that students will use as they explore these resources.

Preparation for Internet Resources: Make sure that you have Adobe Flash, Adobe Shockwave and Java installed on your computers or browsers. These are free and necessary for many of the virtual labs and simulations. You will find links to install these on our resource page - tinyurl.com/ybuwjcnx (password: Matter). Once these have been installed, test out the links for the virtual states of matter labs in unit 3 *Matter and States of Matter*. If you are having trouble, try a different browser such as Google Chrome or Internet Explorer. Still having trouble? View the troubleshooting tips on our resource page, right below the installation links.

Unit presentations can be downloaded or viewed on our resource page. All unit links and research suggestions are also available on the resource page - tinyurl.com/ybuwjcnx (password: Matter).

Lab and Demo Video Alternatives.

For those weeks when you cannot physically complete a lab you can use the links below to still see the lab or demo in action. All links are available on the online resource page: tinyurl.com/ybuwjcnx (password: Matter)

Introduction to Science and Chemistry Labs and Demos
- Burning Bill: tinyurl.com/y95qdwo2
- Mentos and Diet Coke: tinyurl.com/yaqxse8p

Matter and States of Matter Labs and Demos
- Watching Ice Melt Lab:
  Fast Version Time Lapse (1 minute): tinyurl.com/nvqxv5l

Gases and Gas Laws Labs and Demos
- Ivory Soap Demo
- Gas Law Mini Labs:
  - Marshmallow Shrinker (Boyles' Law): tinyurl.com/y73wsw9x
  - A Bunch of Hot Air (Charles' Law): tinyurl.com/ya4e35sf
  - Candle Vacuum (Gay-Lussac's Law): tinyurl.com/ptmyv4u
  - Another Way to Boil Water (Pressure and Boiling Point): tinyurl.com/yahq2q3r
  - Cartesian Diver (Boyle's Law): tinyurl.com/yajetrln
  - Crushed Can (Gay-Lussac's Law): tinyurl.com/ppob6ew

Atoms and Atomic Structure Labs and Demos
- Rainbow Flame Lab: tinyurl.com/ybpdvg69

Physical Properties and Changes Labs and Demos
- Melting Styrofoam Heads Demo: tinyurl.com/ybkhr3lc
- Oobleck Lab: tinyurl.com/y9nc7ucz

Chemical Properties and Changes Labs and Demos
- Burning Steel Wool Demo: tinyurl.com/y83muksw
- Elephant Toothpaste Lab: tinyurl.com/mnm45fj

Acids and Bases Labs and Demos
- Fizzy Drinkable Acid: tinyurl.com/ybtql3lw
- Cabbage Indicator Lab: tinyurl.com/o6zalet
- Acid Attack on Egg Shell: tinyurl.com/ycaz7gvh

Introduction to Science & Chemistry

Intro to Science & Chemistry

Unit One

This week students will practice their science skills, identify safe lab practices and learn about the study of chemistry.

Keywords:

Chemistry	Quantitative Data	Procedure	Independent Variable
Laboratory Safety	Question	Data	Dependent Variable
Scientific Method	Background Research	Conclusion	Physical Reaction
Qualitative Data	Hypothesis	Variables	Chemical Reaction

Day 1—Burning Money, Science Safety Rules, Contract and Oops Lab

Excite your student's interest by lighting a dollar bill on fire only to show that the bill does not burn at all! Explain to them that knowing how chemicals, elements, atoms and molecules work allows us to do all kinds of things. Examples include making plastic, creating life saving medicine and even lighting something on fire without burning it. Quickly explain the science behind the burning money demo and then move on to the next part of the lesson.

Examine the safety rules and contract. Explain to students that it is very important to learn and follow safe lab practices. A safe lab environment means that there will be fewer accidents and injuries, which also means that you can do more exciting and complicated labs. Point out what students should do in case of emergency and where safety equipment is. Students should sign their lab contract and plan to obey safety rules in home and school labs. Lastly, have students use the safety rules to identify the mistakes and misbehaviors happening in the Oops Lab.

Day 2—Mentos and Diet Coke Lab

Use this fun and exciting chemistry lab to teach your students the basics of the scientific method. Students will test diet coke vs regular coke to see which reacts the most with Mentos. We have scaled this experiment down to 20oz bottles of coke and diet coke. Our version is less messy and easier to measure. If you don't mind a little more mess, feel free to substitute a 2-liter bottle of each type of coke and still use 5 Mentos in each bottle. Students will start with a question, form a hypothesis from research, and look at qualitative and quantitative data. They will then graph their independent and dependent variables and write a conclusion. Later in this unit, students will design a simple experiment to test on their own using these steps. Review lab safety and the procedures for this lab. Together discuss the question and give students a moment to write their hypothesis after reading the background research.

Have a level place outside for students to measure the height of their geysers. We recommend using cell phones or cameras to take pictures of the geyser against the measuring tape. Discuss the data students have collected, even having them pool their numbers together and average before graphing. Point out how the independent variable and dependent variables will be placed on the bar graph. Co-op leaders and classroom teachers, you could have half your class bring regular coke and the other half bring diet.

!Big !idea

Design and learn about experimental design using the scientific method. Introduction to the study of Chemistry.

Day 3—What is Chemistry

In this independent activity students will watch the video links and answer questions along the way. Since this is the first day students will be on the computer, we recommend checking your computer to make sure that links are not blocked and that Adobe Flash Player, Adobe Shockwave and Java are installed on your browser or computer. We like to use Google Chrome as our browser but one or two of the virtual labs in this unit work better in Internet Explorer or Safari. Co-op leaders and teachers, you can use a projector to show these videos to the entire class. You might need to repeat a video so that students get all of the information.

Materials:

- **Magnifying Glass or Pocket Microscope**
- **Measuring Tape**
- **Coke, 20 oz at room temp. (save bottle for elephant toothpaste lab)**
- **Diet Coke, 20 oz at room temp.**
- **Index Card**
- **White, Mint Mentos**
- **Dollar Bill**
- **Isopropyl Alcohol, 1/4 cup**
- **Goggles**
- **2 Clear Cups**
- **Salt**
- **Tongs**

Day 4—Scientific Method Experiment Challenge

To actively learn the scientific method students need to do labs and experiments. This week as students learn this important process there will be an extra lab. We certainly encourage students to keep things simple. They could test whether hot water dissolves sugar faster than cold water, whether they kick a ball farther with their right or left leg or test whether skittles or M&Ms bags have more red candies. The point of this lab is for students to design an experiment that they can test. Initial the signature box once they have completed a section correctly and with enough detail (this is a great tool that can be used on other assignments too). Co-op leaders and classroom teachers, we recommend having students design the experiment in class and then test it at home. Discuss each student's results before the quiz tomorrow.

Day 5—QUIZ: Scientific Method and Chemistry Intro

This is a culmination of the week's learning activities. This quiz will cover the scientific method including variables. This quiz will also cover lab safety and hazard symbols. You can have students study their class work. They should pay special attention to the terms in bold. The vocabulary list in your guide can also help them to prepare. The student notebook does not have a copy of the quiz so you will want to make sure you have the quiz ready for them to take.

Next Generation Science Standards—Unit 1

MS-PS1-2: Analyze and interpret data on the properties of substances before and after the substances interact to determine if a chemical reaction has occurred.
4-PS3-4: Apply scientific ideas to design, test, and refine a device that converts energy from one form to another.
5-PS1-4: Conduct an investigation to determine whether the mixing of two or more substances results in new substances.
SC.6-8.N.1.1: Define a problem, use appropriate reference materials to support scientific understanding, plan and carry out scientific investigation of various types, such as systematic observations or experiments, identify variables, collect and organize data, interpret data in charts, tables, and graphics, analyze information, make predictions, and defend conclusions.
SC.7.N.1.4: Identify test variables (independent variables) and outcome variables (dependent variables) in an experiment.

Magic Burning Dollar Demo

A Chemistry Demo

Materials:
- 70% or Higher Isopropyl Rubbing Alcohol
- Salt
- Water
- Tongs
- Measuring Spoons
- Dollar Bill
- Lighter

Caution: This experiment involves fire and heat. Wear safety glasses, use tongs and keep the fire away from flammable items. Have water on hand in case you need to extinguish this small fire.

Preparation:
1. In a cup, mix 1 Tablespoon of warm water with 1/4 teaspoon of table salt.
2. Add 3 Tablespoons of rubbing alcohol to the cup.
3. Soak the dollar bill in this cup for at least 30 seconds. Make sure your dollar bill is completely soaked.

What to Do:
1. Tell students you are going to use the power of chemistry to perform a very special trick.
2. Take the dollar bill out of the alcohol/water solution and gently shake the excess liquid off of it.
3. Move away from the cup of water and alcohol.
4. Hold the dollar bill with tongs and light it on fire.
5. Once the fire is completely extinguished it is safe to touch the dollar bill, which should not have burned at all.
6. As long as you soak the dollar bill again with your alcohol water mixture you can repeat this experiment as many times as you want.

What Happened:
You can do amazing things when you understand chemistry! The secret to lighting a dollar bill on fire without burning it, is the water you used. Evaporating water absorbs the heat energy from the burning alcohol. This keeps the temperature of the dollar bill low enough that it doesn't ignite.

Learning about chemicals and their properties, such as their boiling points and at what temperature they catch fire, allow us to use them for our purposes. In this case, we were able to light a dollar bill on fire without burning it. Even understanding a property such as the color of a chemical's flame can help us. In this lab we added salt, because it burns orange and allows us to really see the fire.

Chemistry is the study of what everything is made of and how it works. As you learn more about chemistry you will have a greater understanding of how our world works.

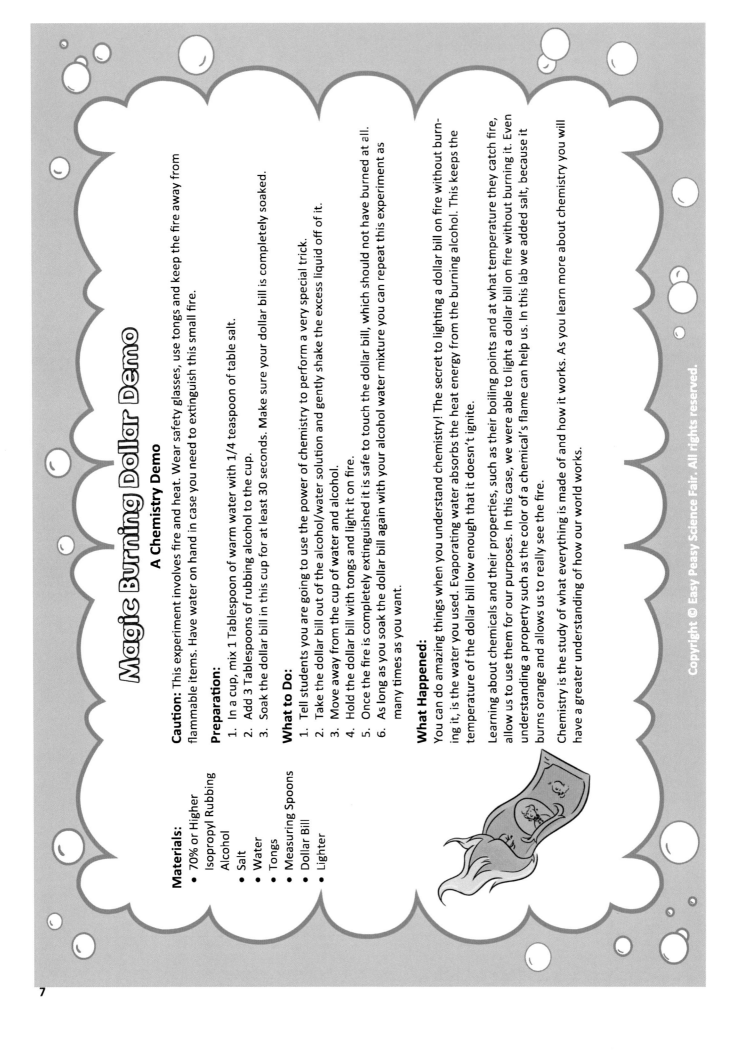

In science, we do a lot of great hands-on labs. It is important to follow these rules to keep yourself and others safe! Safety is always our priority in science class.

1. Read through any instructions or lab procedures before beginning an experiment. Listen carefully to verbal instructions.
2. If you do not understand how to do something, ask for help.
3. Do not play around or run in the lab when doing an experiment.
4. Immediately let your teacher know about unsafe conditions or behaviors you observe.
5. Do not touch equipment or chemicals until you are instructed to do so.
6. Always use science tools the way they should be used.
7. Do not eat or drink anything while completing a lab. Do not eat or drink anything out of your lab equipment.
8. Clean up spilled substances immediately.
9. Never use cracked or broken glass. Inform your teacher or parent if is broken.
10. Label any container you put chemicals in.
11. Never pour liquids into containers held in your hands.
12. Do not look directly into beaker or test tube. Hold up the container and look from the side.
13. Smell a substance by fanning the smell toward you with your hand. Do not put it directly to your nose.
14. Tie back long hair. Wear closed toed shoes. Do not wear loose clothing or jewelry.
15. Wear goggles, apron and gloves when appropriate.
16. Keep hands away from face, eyes, mouth and body while using chemicals or lab equipment.
17. If a chemical gets into your eyes or on your skin, rinse the area for 15 minutes with water.
18. Wash your hands carefully after each activity and after handling chemicals.
19. Keep your work area neat while working.
20. Clean up your area and equipment when you are finished. Put chemicals away correctly and in a safe place where young children cannot reach them.
21. Know what to do and be prepared in case of an emergency. Know the location of safety equipment and the exits. Follow emergency rules and protocol when accidents happen.

Hazard Symbols

Some chemicals can harm us if they are not handled carefully. Hazard symbols are used to identify the danger posed by each chemical and what care should be taken.

 Irritant/Harmful: Skin or respiratory irritation.

 Caution: Blistered skin or rashes.

 Corrosive: Can attack and destroy living tissue, such as skin or bone.

 Toxic: Chemicals which are poisonous and can cause death if they enter the body.

 Flammable: Burn or ignite easily. Must be stored safely and used with care.

 Explosive: Substances have enough stored energy in them that if treated incorrectly may explode.

 High Voltage: Electrical energy at voltages high enough to inflict harm on living organisms.

 Gas under pressure. May be cold when released, and explosive when heated.

Safety Contract

- I have read and understand the science safety rules. I agree to follow them throughout the course of this class.
- I will listen carefully to my teacher and follow all directions.
- I will wear the correct safety equipment when performing experiments.
- I agree to be responsible and to act with caution when performing experiments and activities.

_____   _____
Student Signature   Date

_____   _____
Parent Signature   Date

Oops Lab

Name:

Describe what is wrong with each numbered spot and the lab rule/rules that have been broken. However, one of the students is doing everything right. Which number are they?

1	9
2	10
3	11
4	12
5	13
6	14
7	15
8	16

Mentos and Coke Experiment

Name:

We are going to follow the scientific method as we test the chemistry between Mentos and Coke!

Lab Safety

Goggles and Aprons on!
This can be a messy lab so dress appropriately. This is a good lab to do outside.
Liquid can shoot out of the bottles so it is important to protect your eyes.

Question: Will the reaction between Mentos and regular Coke create a taller geyser than the reaction with Mentos and Diet Coke?

Background Research:

- The original Mint Mentos are round candies with a chewy interior and a hard outer shell. The outside of mint Mentos are covered with many rough small pores because they are sprayed with over 40 microscopic layers of sugar. Gelatin and gum arabic are some of the ingredients in mint Mentos. Mentos are also heavy and will sink in liquid.

- To make your soda bubbly, carbon dioxide is forced into it at extremely high pressures. Diet sodas have slightly more carbonation (carbon dioxide) than regular sodas with different sweeteners.

- Mentos reacting with soda is a **physical reaction**, caused by the small pitted holes on the Mento. The Mento quickly attracts and releases a large amount of the carbon dioxide gas. Because it is heavy and sinks it does this throughout the bottle as it falls. The sudden increase in pressure from the gas being released is what pushes the liquid up and out of the bottle.

- A **Physical Reaction** or **change** can affect the size, shape or color of a substance. The original substance stays the same, no new substance is formed.

Hypothesis: Do you think that there will be a taller geyser from the regular or the diet Coke? Why or why not?

_____

_____

Materials:

2 Cups	Bottle Coke, 20 oz – Room Temp.	Magnifying Glass/Microscope	Measuring Tape
2 Index Cards	Bottle Diet Coke, 20 oz – Room Temp.	Package Mint Mentos	

Procedure:

1. Use your magnifying glass or pocket microscope to observe the exterior of a Mento. Write down your observations.
2. Label your cups: Coke and Diet Coke. Pour a small amount of each type of Coke in the cups.
3. Place one Mento in each cup and observe what happens. Write down your observations, noting any differences or similarities between the two types of sodas.
4. If you are not outside yet, it is a good idea to go outside now. Set up the measuring tape against a wall so that you can measure how high the geyser shoots from each of your bottles of Coke.
5. Place one of your bottles of Coke in front of the measuring tape, on a level surface.
6. Roll your paper to make a tube. Line up 5 of your Mentos in the tube, in a stack.
7. Cover the bottom of the tube with another index card and place it over your bottle of soda.
8. Make sure that your tube is right over the top of your bottle so that the Mentos will drop in once the index card is removed. Now, quickly slide the index card out so that the Mentos all drop into the Coke at once.
9. Get out of the way! This is a wet zone, so expect to get wet!
10. Observe and record how high the geyser reached on your measuring tape and then repeat steps 5-9 with your other Coke.

Data Tables:

Qualitative Data:

Qualitative data describes something. In an experiment, it is what you can see or notice but cannot measure in numbers. (Hint: think quality for description.)

Observations	
Mentos	
Diet Coke	
Regular Coke	
Mentos + Diet Coke	
Mentos + Regular Coke	

Quantitative Data:

Quantitative data can be counted or measured. It can be measured in numbers. (Hint: think quantity for numbers.)

	Height of Geyser
Diet Coke	
Regular Coke	

Graph:

Create a bar graph to compare how high the geyser of each type of Coke was. In science, it is always better to use the metric system when measuring. But since many United States measuring tapes are only in inches, it is okay if you used inches to measure for this lab.

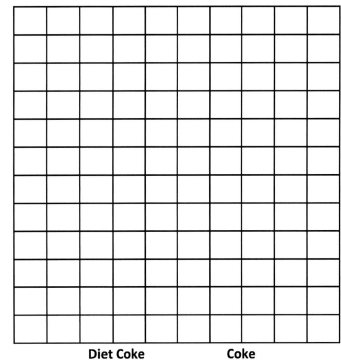

Your INDEPENDENT VARIABLE (what you are testing) goes on the X-Axis.

Conclusion:

On another sheet of paper, use your data and observations to write whether your hypothesis was supported or not supported. By the way, an unsupported (not proven) hypothesis is perfectly okay! Discuss why you think you got the results you did. Also, include what you might have done better and another experiment you might do based upon this lab.

Name:

There are so many fantastic free learning videos on the internet. Answer the questions on this sheet as you watch the following videos. You might need to rewatch these short videos once or twice, to answer all the questions.

Importance of Chemistry in Life (3:03 min)

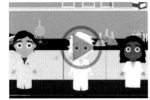

Go to: tinyurl.com/por7sek

1. When we eat breathe or just sit down what is taking place?

2. Chemistry is the study of _____.

3. What are 3 examples of chemical reactions?

4. What are 3 important uses of chemistry?

5. What is something that people used to die from?

6. What can studying chemicals help us to do?

Chemistry Life Hacks (3:47 min)

Go to: tinyurl.com\kor3j5

1. What is built up in an egg as it goes bad?

2. What about an onion reacts to make your eyes tear? What is the fix?

3. What gets replaced in veggies, causing them to lose their bright green color?

Importance of Chemistry in Life (3:03 min)

Go to: tinyurl.com/oyrbyop

1. What is the most exciting phrase to hear in science?

2. What were the chemicals in coal tar similar to?

3. Instead of Aspirin what did Perkin end up discovering? Why was this a big deal?

4. Because of Perkin what sprang up trying to make treasure out of trash? How is this a good thing?

5. What did Fahlberg discover by not washing his hands?

6. Fluorinated hydrocarbons led Plunkett to discover _____. What was it good for?

7. Because Teflon didn't stretch well. Bob's frustration allowed him to discover what?

Got More Time? Extra Video:
Chemical Curiosities: Surprising Science (1:09:42)

Go to: tinyurl.com/kqrvjrc

Watch these fantastic demonstrations from the Royal Institution. For each demo you watch, **write down what the demo was and the science behind it**. You can do this on the back of this paper if it is blank or on another sheet of paper.

Scientific Method Experiment Challenge

You are going to use the scientific method as you design a simple experiment. You will test the experiment yourself. The purpose of this assignment is to give you practice when experimenting. Pick something simple to test that you can finish in 1-2 days max! If you are a little confused about the scientific method, try watching this Science Jam video: tinyurl.com/7ukupju

Ask a Question ⟩ Research ⟩ Hypothesis ⟩ Test Hypothesis ⟩ Analyze Data Draw a Conclusion ⟩ Share Your Findings

What will you test?

There are many simple questions you could design an experiment around. If you still have extra coke and Mentos you could even further explore this topic. Do more Mentos make a larger geyser? Do other diet sodas work just as well? Here are some other simple ideas you could test, but do not feel like you have to stick to this list. If you are wondering about something else than go ahead and explore it with permission from your teacher or parent!

Simple Ideas

- Which side of a penny holds more drops of water?
- What style of paper airplane will fly the farthest?
- Which type of bubble gum has the longest lasting flavor?
- Can you add something to ice water to make it colder?

List your Question on the lines below:

Parent/Teacher Initials

Variables:

Whenever you complete an experiment, you have a variable that you test or change on purpose, which is the independent variable. You will also have a variable you will measure to see your results: the dependent variable. The control group is to see if what you are testing makes a difference. All the other variables must be kept the same in order for the experiment to be fair, which are the controlled variables.

	Example from Mentos Diet Coke Experiment	**Your Variables**
Independent Variable	Regular Coke	
Dependent Variable	Height of the Geyser	
Control Group	Diet Coke	
Controlled Variables	Same amount of Coke Same number of Mentos Measuring tool used the same way	

Background Research:

Look up information on your topic. Make sure to read at least two sources. Write what you have learned in the space below.

Hypothesis:

Now that you have some background knowledge, write down what you think the results of your experiment will be.

_____

_____

Materials:

Procedure:

Write a detailed procedure in the lines below. Use as many lines as necessary.:

1.	
2.	
3.	
4.	
5.	
6.	
7.	
8.	
9.	
10.	
11.	
12.	
13.	
12.	
13.	
14.	

Data Tables:

BEFORE beginning your experiment, draw your data tables, on another paper. It is always important to know how you will collect your data ahead of time. It is also important to collect data in an organized way so that you do not get confused.

Graph:

Compare your data by creating a graph, on another sheet of paper. Make sure you label your graph correctly.

Conclusion:

On another sheet of paper use your data and observations, to write down whether your hypothesis was supported or not supported. Discuss why you think you got the results you did. Also, include what you might have done better and another experiment you might do based upon this lab.

Scientific Method and Safety Quiz

Name:

True/False
Indicate whether the statement is true or false.

_____ 1. You should always carefully read the instructions before starting an experiment.

_____ 2. Never reach across an open flame.

_____ 3. Broken, chipped, or cracked glassware can be used as long as it doesn't leak.

_____ 4. You should inform your teacher immediately if you spill or splash chemicals on your skin, cut or burn yourself, or get something in your eye.

_____ 5. You should wear your safety glasses only when you are working with chemicals, open flames, or substances that may be harmful to your eyes.

Matching
Please match the correct hazard symbol with what it stands for.

a.   b.   c.   d.   e.

_____ 6. Corrosive   _____ 7. Caution   _____ 8. Toxic   _____ 9. Flammable   _____ 10. High Voltage

Multiple Choice
Identify the choice that best completes the statement or answers the question.

_____ 11. Why is it important to obey safety rules?
- a. It isn't important to obey rules, because they slow you down.
- b. because your teacher says it's important
- c. to prevent accidents and avoid injury if an accident does happen
- d. to make you learn more about science

_____ 12. Which scientific investigation does **not** include dependent and independent variables?
- a. Studying the effect of enzymes in laundry detergent on stains.
- b. Testing boats to see if raising the engine makes them faster.
- c. counting squirrel populations

_____ 13. Scientific investigations include many different steps. During a scientific investigation, which step occurs after a scientist collects and analyzes the data?
- a. Draw conclusions
- b. Form the hypothesis
- c. Plan the experiment
- d. Background research

_____ 14. Lindsey finds that the data from her experiment does not support her hypothesis. What should she do?
- a. Change the procedure to get a different result.
- b. Change the data to fit the hypothesis.
- c. Plan a new experiment to investigate it.
- d. Hide her results.

_____ 15. Identify the Independent Variable: Will baking soda make my cake rise more than baking powder?
- a. The independent variable is not listed.
- b. How much the cake rises
- c. Baking Soda
- d. Baking Soda and Baking Powder

_____ 16. Identify the Dependent Variable in this experiment: Will I ollie higher on a long or a short skateboard?
- a. How high I ollie
- b. The shortboard
- c. The dependent variable is not listed.
- d. The shortboard and the longboard

_____ 17. Cameron completed an experiment by looking at how temperature affected the reaction time of baking soda and vinegar. He recorded how long each reaction took. He then created this table to show his results. What is the **main** problem with Cameron's table?

How Temperature Affects the Reaction Time of Baking Soda and Vinegar

Beaker	Temperature	Time
A	0	8
B	30	5
C	50	2
D	100	.5

- a. The units are missing.
- b. He didn't repeat the experiment enough times.
- c. The values are incorrect.
- d. The title is incorrect.

Oops Lab
1. There is food and a mess in the lab. Rules broken: 7,8
2. Not wearing goggles, beaker is cracked. She is also holding the container she is pouring into. Rules broken: 9,11,15
3. Goofing around in the lab and using science tools to play around. Rules broken:6, 3
4. There is a backpack left on the lab table. Rules broken: 19
5. Not wearing goggles and is just dropping papers on the ground. Rules broken: 15,19
6. Drinking out of an Erlenmeyer flask. Rules broken:6,7
7. Student is doing everything right. Rules broken: none
8. Smelling the substance in the beaker. Rules broken: 13
9. Long hair isn't tied back and could get into the petri dish she is working with. Rules broken: 14
10. Messy work area. Rules broken: 8,19
11. Aprons were left or dropped on the ground. Rules broken: 20
12. Head is in the fume hood. Rules broken: 6
13. Running while on fire. Rules broken: 21
14. Boxes under the safety shower prevent students who need to use it. Rules broken: 21
15. Pouring chemicals down the sink. Rules broken:20
16. Isn't wearing closed toed shoes or goggles. Rules broken: 14

Mentos and Coke Experiment
<u>Hypothesis</u>: should discuss whether diet coke or regular coke will create a larger geyser and why they think so. Answers will vary.
<u>Qualitative observations</u>: Students should describe what they see and notice about each item.
<u>Quantitative Data</u>: Should include the height of their geyser in diet and regular coke. Students should include the unit.
Example: Diet Coke: 11 inches; Regular Coke: 5 inches
<u>Example Bar Graph</u>:

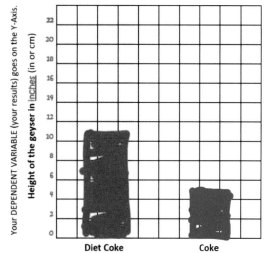

<u>Example Conclusion</u>: My hypothesis that the regular coke would have a higher geyser was not supported. The geyser of the diet coke and mentos was 11 inches high while the geyser from the regular coke was 5 inches. I think that this happened because diet sodas have more carbonation to react with the mint mentos. I could have done a better job at getting the mentos into the coke at the same time. If I were to continue this experiment, I would test whether different types of mentos make a difference in the height of the geyser.
<u>**Explanation**</u>: the 40 microscopic layers of sugar that are sprayed onto each mento creates a lot of nooks and crannies for nucleation to happen. Nucleation is a <u>physical reaction </u>where the gas (carbon dioxide) in the soda grabs onto the bumps and nooks on the mento to form bubbles. As the mentos fall to the bottom of the soda bottle more and more bubbles are quickly turned into a raging foam. This builds the pressure and the gas bursts out of the bottle creating a geyser!

What is Chemistry Videos
1: Importance of chemistry in life
1. Chemical Reaction
2. Everything

→

3. Raw meat cooking, baking a cake, rotting and the way we store food
4. Cleaning, cooking, medicine
5. Common Cold
6. Discover ways to produce chemicals that are not harmful to the natural world.

2: Chemistry Life Hacks
1. Gases
2. Amino acid sulfoxides form when a knife slices an onion, this gas reacts with the water in your eyes, burning them and causing your eyes to release tears to wash the irritant away.
3. Chlorophyll loses a magnesium atom. Don't cook them as long

3: Accidental Chemistry Discoveries that Changed the World
1. That's funny...
2. Aspirin
3. Purple dye; before this purple dye was so expensive that only the rich could wear it. Now the middle class could afford to wear colors like purple.
4. Because he was so successful and became so wealthy, many new chemical research plants came about and many good things were discovered because of them.
5. Saccharin
6. Teflon; nonstick surface
7. He angrily yanked hot Teflon and it stretched, making a light and bendable fiber. This is used to make rain coats. We call it goretex.

Scientific Method Experiment Challenge
Answers will vary for this experiment. Initial each section once students have satisfactorily completed it.
Example Experiment: Will my right leg kick a soccer ball the furthest?
Variables:
<u>Independent Variable</u>: should be the variable being tested. Example: right leg used to kick
<u>Dependent Variable</u>: is the result, the variable being measured. Example: how far the ball was kicked
<u>Control Group</u>: This group is used to compare. It makes sure that the independent variable is tested against something. Example: left leg used to kick (this way we can see if the right leg actually kicked farther.)
<u>Controlled Variables</u>: This is everything that is kept the same, so that the experiment is fair. Example: Angle of kick, same ball used, same player kicking, etc.
Background Research: Students should use at least 2 sources.
Hypothesis and Materials will vary.
Procedure will vary but should be detailed enough so that someone could use just the written procedure to perform the experiment.
Look at the data tables for the Coke and Mentos experiment to see where the variables should be on the graph and how it should be labeled.
Conclusions will vary, but should use data and observations, should include whether the hypothesis was supported or not supported. Discuss results and why they were what they were. What might have been done better and an idea for another extension experiment should be included.

Scientific Method and Safety Quiz
1. True
2. True
3. False
4. True
5. False
6. B
7. C
8. E
9. A
10. D
11. C
12. C
13. A
14. C
15. C
16. A

Matter
& Its States

SOLID
LIQUID
GAS

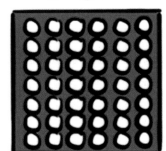

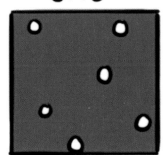

Matter & Its States

This week students will learn the basics about matter and its states. They will start to understand that particle movement affects state of matter.

Keywords:

Solid	Boiling	Pressure	Heating Curve
Liquid	Condensing	Freezing Point	Density
Gas	Melting	States of Matter	Mass
Plasma	Sublimation	Compression	Weight
Particles	Evaporation	Viscosity	Matter
Freezing	Crystalline	Electrons	Kinetic Energy

Day 1—Matter Notes

Understanding the differences between the 4 states of matter gives students great insight into the way particle movement affects the state of matter. What causes a substance to change state shows how so many things in our world work. On this day students will learn about the different states of matter and what causes substances to change state. You will find the presentation on our Resource page tinyurl.com/ybuwjcnx (password: Matter). You can download the PowerPoint file and give the presentation yourself or you can use the recorded presentation. A student can watch the recorded presentation on their own to fill out their notes as they learn about the states of matter.

Day 2—Watching Ice Melt Lab

Looking at the temperature as ice melts and then begins to boil might seem like a strange thing to do. Surprisingly this lab keeps students busy and shows them what a heat curve is. The temperature of a cup of ice will increase until the ice starts to melt. The temperature stops rising and will stay the same as the ice melts and begins to go through a phase change. This is because the heat energy is being used to melt the ice. Once all of the ice is melted the temperature will begin to rise again until the water begins to turn to a gas, as it evaporates. When energy is used for a phase change the temperature stays the same (constant). This rate of temperature rising looks like a curve on a graph, which is why we call it a heat curve. You will need a heat source for this lab such as a stove or hot plate. Students will see the heating curve of water as it changes states. If you are grouping students we recommend groups of only 2 students, 3 max. If you only have one heat source and are working with a class or group have students come up to take turns watching the thermometer.

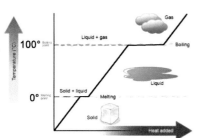

!Big !idea *Matter may undergo changes of state (solid, liquid, gas and plasma). All matter has mass and volume.*

Day 3—Matter Labs (Online)

Students love doing online labs and it is a great way for them to try their hand at things that aren't easy to do in the classroom or at home. There are three virtual labs to complete and one short video on states of matter. You can break this activity into two days if you do not have 45 minutes to work or if your student needs more time. As long as Adobe flash player and Java are installed, all of these activities should work. You can also try a different browser (google chrome, internet explorer or firefox) if you are having trouble. All of the sites are safe to visit. Co-op leaders and teachers can project these labs and work through them as a class. We like to have students take turns to complete each task while everyone fills out the handout together.

Materials:
- Clear Cup
- Goggles
- Heat Source
- Thermometer
- Timer (can use phone)
- Ice

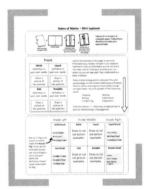

Day 4—States of Matter: Mini Lapbook

In this hands on activity, students will make a mini lapbook or fold-it to illustrate the four states of matter. We recommend giving each student an 8.5x11 sheet of paper for this and 4 post-its. Students will also need scissors and glue or tape. Students can use their notes and work, the internet, books and encyclopedias to look up images and definitions. For convenience, we have provided images and arrows but students can draw their own images or get them from another source.

Day 5—QUIZ: Matter and its States

This is a culmination of the week's learning activities. This quiz will cover the 4 states of matter and their properties as well as particle movement.. You can have students study their class work. They should pay special attention to the terms in bold. The vocabulary list in your guide can also help them to prepare. The student notebook does not have a copy of the quiz so you will want to make sure you have the quiz ready for them to take.

Next Generation Science Standards—Unit 2

MS-PS1-3: Make observations and measurements to identify materials based on their properties.
MS-PS3-4: Plan an investigation to determine the relationships among the energy transferred, the type of matter, the mass, and the change in the average kinetic energy of the particles as measured by the temperature of the sample.
MS-PS1-4: Develop a model that predicts and describes changes in particle motion, temperature, and state of a pure substance when thermal energy is added or removed.
MS-PS1-4a: Changes of state that occur with variations in temperature or pressure can be described and predicted using these models of matter.
Cross Cutting Concept-Scale, Proportion and Quantity: Standard units are used to measure and describe physical quantities such as weight, time, temperature, and volume.

States of Matter Student Notes   Name:

Matter

- Takes up _____, and has _____.
- _____ states of matter
- Made up of _____ that are _____ in motion. _____ down as they get _____
- _____ is determined by how much _____ a particle has (_____ energy)

Solid
Draw Particles:

- Have a _____ _____
- Have a _____ _____
- Arranged in _____ regular _____ and move very _____.
- _____ packed

Liquid
Draw Particles:

- Have a _____ volume but _____ definite _____.
- _____ tightly _____ than solids.
- _____ _____ past each other and change _____ to fill _____.

Gas
Draw Particles:

- Has no _____ _____.
- Has _____ fixed _____.
- Particles move _____.
- _____ _____ between particles.

Plasma
Draw Particles:

- Is _____ gas.
- _____ electrons stream through _____ _____.
- Has _____ fixed _____ or _____.
- Conducts _____ and is affected by _____ _____.
- _____ of universe is composed of _____!

Watching Ice Melt

This might seem like a strange lab to do, BUT it will teach you something important about temperature and states of matter.

Lab Safety **Goggles and Aprons on!**
You will be working around a heat source and boiling water.
This lab should only be done under adult supervision.

Question: How will increasing the heat affect the state of H_2O?

Background Research: The first law of thermodynamics states that energy can be transformed, but cannot be created or destroyed. This leads into the concept of how different substances can change from one phase to another by absorbing or releasing energy. In an **endothermic** phase change a substance gains heat energy. In an **exothermic** phase change a substance releases energy into the environment. When the system is heated, it changes by increasing its temperature. A plot of the temperature versus time is called the heating curve.

Hypothesis: Use what you know about water to write your hypothesis.

_____

_____

Materials:

Ice	Beaker or Pot	Thermometer with Range:	Heat Source: Stove, Hot Plate,
Timer (can use phone)	Cup	0°C- 100°C or 30°F-212°F	Bunsen Burner, etc

Imagine you put the following substances in hot water. Predict what will happen to them.

Substance	In Hot Water it Will...
Butter	
Rock	
Chocolate	
Dry Ice	

Intro Activity: Imagine you put an ice cube in a cup of lukewarm water. What do you think will happen to the ice cube? What do you think will happen to the temperature of the water?

1. Fill a cup or beaker half full with warm water then measure and record the water temperature under beginning temperature for Ice Cube #1.
2. Set a timer as you add an ice cube to the water. Gently stir it with your thermometer until the ice cube melts. Now record the time it took for the ice cube to melt and the temperature of the water under Ice Cube #1.
3. Immediately add a second ice cube to the water. Set your timer and then stir this ice cube until it melts. Now record the melting time and ending temperature of the water as soon as it melts.

Ice Cube Number	Beginning Temperature	Ending Temperature	Melting Time
1			
2			

4. Which of the ice cubes melted fastest? Why do you think it took longer for one of the ice cubes to melt?

5. Do you think if you put an ice cube in hotter water that it would melt at a different rate than if you put the ice cube in colder water?

Procedure

1. Fill your small pot or glass beaker with ice.
2. Suspend the thermometer in your container so that it does not touch the bottom. Depending upon your thermometer there are a few ways to do this. If your thermometer already has a clip you can use that. Otherwise you can use a thermometer clamp or a clothes pin.
3. Record the starting temperature of your ice and the state it is in (S:Solid, L:Liquid, G:Gas) in your data table.
4. You will now turn on your heat source and start your timer. For a stove or a hotplate, you would turn it on high.
5. Every 30 seconds you will record the state and temperature of your container.
6. Continue until your temperature has stopped changing at the boiling point.

Data Table:

Time (min.)	S/L/G	Temp: °C or °F	Time (min.)	S/L/G	Temp: °C or °F	Time (min.)	S/L/G	Temp: °C or °F
0.0								
0.5								
1.0								

Graph

Create a line graph of your data that includes the following:

- Label the x-axis with the time (in minutes).
- Label the y-axis as temperature (in degrees either Fahrenheit or Celsius).
- Create a title for your graph that describes the data.
- Color your line to show what state your water was in. Blue while it was a solid, yellow for liquid and red for gas. Also label the following points on your graph: MP (Melting Point) and BP (Boiling Point).

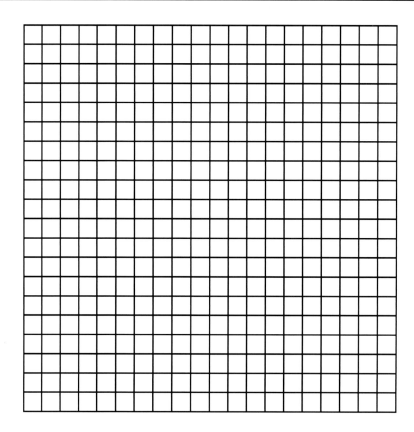

Conclusion and Analysis:

1. How did adding heat energy affect the state of your water?

2. Were the phase changes you observed today exothermic or endothermic?

3. Explain what was happening to the water molecules in the flat areas of your graph.

4. Explain what was happening to the water molecules in the sloped areas of your graph.

5. If you were adding thermal energy the whole time, why were there times when the temperature did not change much? (What was the thermal energy during those periods?)

6. When the water was boiling, was it releasing energy or absorbing energy? Explain your answer.

7. If you put liquid water in the freezer would it be absorbing or releasing heat as it froze? Explain your answer.

8. Look at this graph of a waxy material called Lauric Acid. At what temperature does Lauric acid change from a solid to a liquid? Explain your answer.

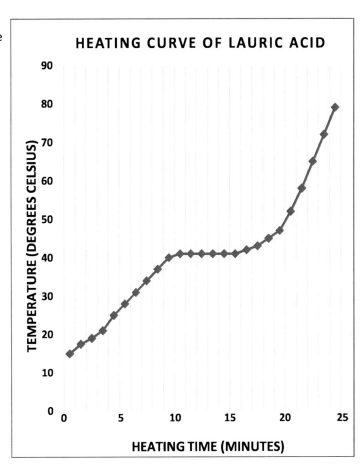

Matter Labs

There are so many fantastic free activities and interactive labs online. Answer the questions on this sheet as you explore these activities and online labs.

Basic Solid and Liquids Exploration

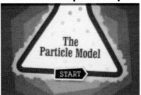

Go to: tinyurl.com/nw9872v

1.   This interactive presentation lets you try to compress and change the shapes of solids, liquids and gases.

2.   In a solid how are particles held together?

3.   In a liquid the particles are still held together but what are they able to do?

	Solid	Liquid	Gas
Could you change its shape?			
Why?			
Could you compress it?			
Why?			
3 Examples of the State			
Why are these properties useful?			

Properties of Matter Study Jam

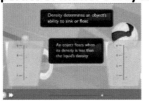

Go to: tinyurl.com/7f5t8l3 -Choose play video.

1.   Why is a golf ball heavier than a much larger beach ball?

2.   What is Density? What is its formula?

3.   List 4 properties of Matter:

4.   Define Mass.

5.   How are Mass and Weight different?

6.   Define Volume.

7.   What is the trick for measuring the volume of things that cannot be measured with a ruler?

8.   Why does a golf ball sink in water while a beach ball floats?

States of Matter Interactive

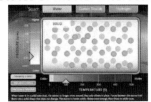

Go to: tinyurl.com/cqbjz92 – Launch Interactive

Water is the only substance on Earth that occurs naturally as a solid, liquid and a gas. Scientists can artificially transform other substances by manipulating their temperature and pressures. In this lab you will get to play with 3 substances: Water, Carbon Dioxide and Hydrogen, to see how you can change their particle movement and states.

Once on this page. Launch the interactive.
1. Select Water and slide the pressure up to 1 atm.
2. Select to "View temp in Fahrenheit".
3. Slide the temperature scale until the water enters a liquid state. Write this temperature in Fahrenheit _____ and in Celsius _____
4. Continue to slide the scale until the water enters a gaseous state. Write this temperature in Fahrenheit _____ and in Celsius _____
5. Without touching the temperature can you change this water back to a liquid or a solid by adjusting the pressure? Explain what you did why you think you got your results.

6. Fill out this data table with the state of the particles at each temperature. Adjust the pressure to 1 atm for both substances.

Water					
Carbon Dioxide					
Temperature	-279.7 F -173 C	-99.7 F -73 C	80.3 F 27 C	260.3 F 127 C	440.3 F 227 C

7. At 0.1 atm is there a difference in the Carbon Dioxide atoms when you change the temperature from 260.3 F to 440.3 F?

8. How would you say that temperature and pressure relate to the movement and state of a particle?

9. Can you find a way to make Carbon Dioxide a liquid? Can you come up with an explanation for this?

10. Look at the temperature gauge for Hydrogen. How is it different than the gauge for Water and Carbon Dioxide? Why do you think they did this?

11. Play around with the Hydrogen atom. Can you get it into a very special 5th state of matter? How did you do this?

12. What is "BEC"? Draw and define it.

Solid, Liquid, Gas Quick Lab

Go to: tinyurl.com/2nfdaw

Draw and describe the particle movement for each state of matter:

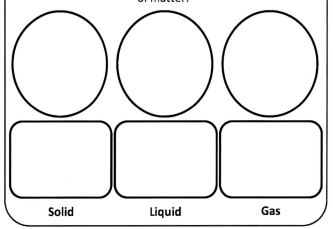

| Solid | Liquid | Gas |

States of Matter – Mini Lapbook

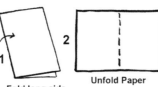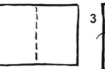

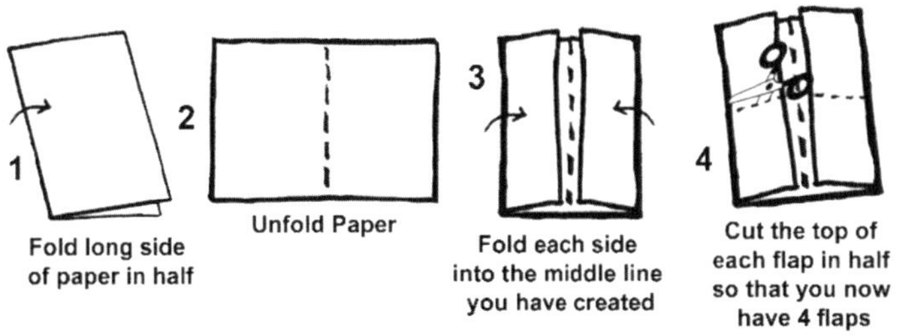

1. Fold long side of paper in half

2. Unfold Paper

3. Fold each side into the middle line you have created

4. Cut the top of each flap in half so that you now have 4 flaps

Take an 8.5 x 11 piece of computer paper. Follow these directions to make your lapbook folds.

Front

SOLID	Liquid
Definition in your own words.	Definition in your own words.
Draw a picture of the particles	Draw a picture of the particles
GAS	**PLASMA**
Definition in your own words.	Definition in your own words.
Draw a picture of the particles	Draw a picture of the particles

Look at the pictures on this page to see what information you need to include in your lapbook. Feel free to look up information you do not know. Just make sure to write your answers your own words! As you can see, each flap is dedicated to a State of Matter.

Place or draw energy arrows between the solid, liquid and gas on the inside middle of your foldable. Place an arrow showing how these states change into each other. You will use each of the following words:

Freezing	Melting
Boiling	Sublimation
Condensing	Evaporation

Color the arrows blue that show energy being lost and red where energy is being gained.

Inside Left   Inside Middle   Inside Right

We cut 3 flaps into a post-it note to make this **Vocab Flip**. If you do not have post-its you can cut and tape a piece of paper. Write the definition of each word underneath its flap.

Solid Vocab

Crystalline

Pressure

Freezing Point

Gas Vocab

Compression

Evaporation

Sublimation

SOLID

Draw or cut out picture examples.

GAS

Draw or cut out picture examples.

Liquid

Draw or cut out picture examples.

PLASMA

Draw or cut out picture examples.

Liquid Vocab

Viscosity

Melting Point

Condensation

Plasma Vocab

Ions

Electrons

Northern Lights

States of Matter – Mini Lapbook

You can cut and paste these images and words into your lapbook OR you can draw or find your own!

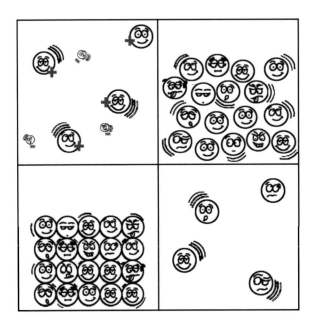

SOLID
LIQUID
GAS
PLASMA

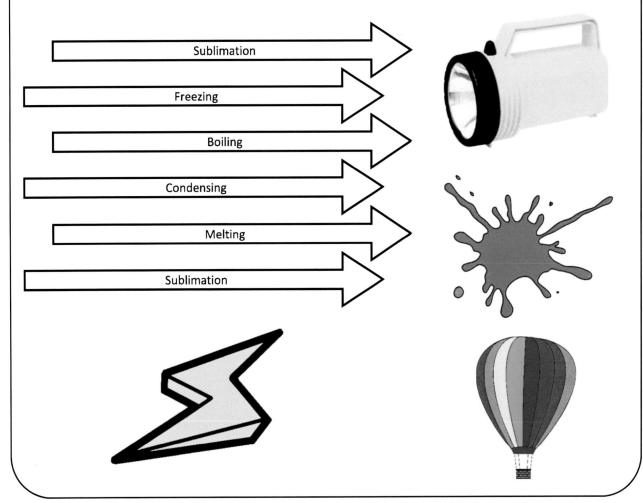

Sublimation

Freezing

Boiling

Condensing

Melting

Sublimation

States of Matter Quiz

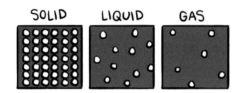

Name: _____

SOLID   LIQUID   GAS

Multiple Choice

Identify the choice that best completes the statement or answers the question.

_____ 1. The basic building blocks of matter are _____.
a. neutrons.   b. atoms.   c. electrons.   d. protons.

_____ 2. An ice cube that melts into liquid water is an example of_____.
a. a change in composition.   b. reactivity.   c. a change of identity.   d. a change of state.

_____ 3. What kind of energy decides whether carbon dioxide is solid, liquid, or gas?
a. potential energy   b. kinetic energy   c. physical energy   d. chemical energy

_____ 4. The formula *length x width x height* is used to measure _____.
a. weight.   b. mass.   c. volume.   d. matter.

_____ 5. Why is 1 kg of lead easier to carry around all day than 1 kg of feathers?
a. Lead has less mass but less density than feathers.   b. Lead has more mass but less density than feathers.   c. Lead has less mass but more density than feathers.   d. Lead has the same mass but more density than feathers.

_____ 6. Water is a liquid at 40° Celsius. What could make water a solid at this same temperature?
a. Pressure   b. mass   c. heat   d. nothing

_____ 7. What law says that energy cannot be created or destroyed, only changed?
a. 2nd law of conservation of mass   b. the law of conservation of entropy   c. the law of conservation of matter   d. 1st law of thermodynamics

_____ 8. The graph above shows the heating curve of an acid. At what temperature is this acid a liquid?
a. 40°C   b. 0°C   c. 150°C   d. 300°C

Matching

Match <u>one or more </u>of the choices that best complete the statement or answer the question.

a. Plasma   b. Gas   c. Solid   d. Liquid   e. Weight
f. Mass   g. Volume   h. Density   i. Matter   j. Kinetic

_____ 9. Can be compressed

_____ 10. Amount of space taken up by something

_____ 11. Not a solid or liquid and can conduct electricity

_____ 12. Has a fixed volume but no fixed shape

_____ 13. Has a fixed volume

_____ 14. If something has mass and takes up space

_____ 15. The amount of matter in an object

_____ 16. Particles have the most energy and movement

Answer Key—Unit 2: Matter & Its States

Matter Notes
Matter
- Space; Volume
- Four
- Particles; Always; Slow; Colder
- State; Energy; Kinetic

Solid

- Fixed Volume
- Fixed Shape
- Tight; Pattern; Slowly
- Tightly

Liquid

- Fixed; No, Shape
- Less; Packed
- Particles slide; Shape; Container

Gas
- Fixed shape
- No; Volume
- Rapidly
- Large Spaces

Plasma
- Ionized
- Negative; Positive ions
- No; Shape; Volume
- Electricity; Magnetic Fields
- 99%; Plasma

Watching Ice Melt Experiment
Hypothesis: should discuss what student knows about water and heat to hypothesize how heat will affect the state of H₂O.
Substance Predictions: Answers will vary. Example: Melt; Feel warm; Melt; Boil and turn to gas
Intro Activity answers will vary. Example:

Ice Cube Number	Beginning Temperature	Ending Temperature	Melting Time
1	102°	89.6°	1 min 19 sec
2	89.6°	77°	1 min 59 sec

4. The first ice cube melted fastest. Answers will vary but the greater the temperature difference the faster the heat exchange between the water and the ice.
5. Student answers will vary but an ice cube will melt faster in hotter water because the greater the temperature difference the faster the heat exchange between two substances.

Procedure Data Table(Sample Answers):

Time (min)	S/L/G	Temp: °C or °F	Time (min)	S/L/G	Temp: °C or °F	Time (min)	S/L/G	Temp: °C or °F
0.0	S	5°	7.5	L	64°	15.0	L	204°
0.5	S/L	14°	8.0	L	76°	15.5	L	207°
1.0	S/L	23°	8.5	L	90°	16.0	L	209°
1.5	S/L	32°	9.0	L	98°	16.5	L	211°
2.0	S/L	32°	9.5	L	108°	17.0	L/G Boiling	212°
2.5	S/L	32°	10.0	L	118°	17.5	L/G Boiling	212°
3.0	S/L	32°	10.5	L	129°	18.0	L/G Boiling	212°
3.5	S/L	32°	11.0	L	137°	18.5	L/G Boiling	212°
4.0	S/L	32°	11.5	L	147°	19.0	L/G Boiling	212°
4.5	S/L	32°	12.0	L	154°	19.5	L/G Boiling	212°
5.0	L	33°	12.5	L	164°	20.0	L/G Boiling	212°
5.5	L	35°	13.0	L	175°	20.5	L/G Boiling	212°
6.0	L	38°	13.5	L	183°	21.0	L/G Boiling	212°
6.5	L	45°	14.0	L	191°	21.5	L/G Boiling	212°
7.0	L	55°	14.5	L	198°	22.0	L/G Boiling	212°

→

Sample Line Graph:

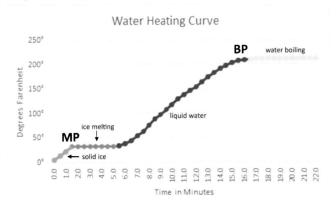

Conclusion and Analysis
1. It caused the water to change state.
2. Endothermic, because the water was absorbing the heat energy.
3. In the flat areas of the graph the water was going through a phase or state change. It was not completely a solid, liquid or a gas.
4. In the sloped areas of my graph the water was one state or phase and the temperature was rising.
5. During the flat times the energy was being used to change the state or phase of the water and so we didn't see the temperature rise.
6. Water is absorbing energy which is why it was going into the gaseous state. The absorbed energy makes the particles move fast enough to be in the gaseous state/phase.
7. It would be releasing energy, causing the particles to have less energy and to move less which is why the water freezes into a solid state.
8. It changes from a solid to a liquid at 40°. You can tell this because the graph is flat and begins to rise again at 40°.

Matter Labs Online
1: Basic Solid and Liquids Exploration
1. Powerful forces called BONDS.
2. Flow

	Solid	Liquid	Gas
Change its shape?	No	Yes	Yes
Why?	The bonds hold them together.	Flow even with strong bonds that keep them together.	They have no bonds
Compress it?	No	No	Yes
Why?	So squished together, no place for them to go.	The particles are so close together	So far apart you can push them closer together.
3 Examples	Steel, bricks and wood	Water, Milk and Petrol	Oxygen, Helium and Nitrogen
Why are these properties useful?	Because it keeps its shape and cannot be compressed we can build things like houses with solids.	Since it doesn't keep its shape but stays together, it flows. Use this to send liquid through pipes, like a toilet.	One reason is that we can contain it and because we can compress it we can have comfortable air mattresses.

2: Properties of Matter Study Jam
1. It is more dense
2. The measure of how light or heavy something is for its size.

$$Density = \frac{mass}{volume}$$

3. Mass, Weight, Volume, Density
4. The amount of matter in an object
5. Weight measures the force of gravity on a mass. It can change depending upon where it is. Mass is the measure of how much a substance is. It doesn't change depending upon where it is.
6. The amount of space an object takes up.
7. Measure with water. Drop it in and see how high the water rises.
8. Because the golf ball is denser than the water and the beach ball is les dense than water.

3: States of Matter Interactive
3. 80.3°; 27°
4. 260.3° ; 127°
5. By raising the pressure to 10, I was able to change the water to a liquid. There was not enough pressure to change it to a solid at this temperature. I think that raising the pressure helps the particles stay together even if they have enough energy to be in another state.

Water	Solid	Solid	Liquid	Gas	Gas
Carbon Dioxide	Solid	Gas	Gas	Gas	Gas
Temp.	-279.7 F	-99.7 F-	80.3 F	260.3 F	440.3 F

7. Yes, the particles move faster.
8. The greater the temperature the more speed/energy a particle has, but the greater the pressure the less speed/energy a particle has and it can stay bonded to the other particles as a solid or a liquid.
9. No. It is hard to do small changes in the temperature and pressure, there is probably a small window where Carbon Dioxide is a liquid, under the right pressure and temperature.
10. The hottest it gets is a hundred degrees less than the coldest the water and carbon dioxide get. I think the temperature is different because hydrogen is a gas at really low temperatures. Its bonds must not be strong enough to keep it together.
12. In this state of matter the atoms exist in the same space with the same amount of energy. Because the atoms are in the same place it is sometimes called a super atom. They come very close to not moving.

4: Solid, Liquid, Gas Quick Lab

Particles of a solid are arranged in a tight regular pattern, and move very little.

The particles of a liquid move past each other easily. They are close together, but not in a neat arrangement.

The particles of a gas move rapidly and there are much larger spaces between them than between the particles in a liquid or solid.

States of Matter– Mini Lapbook
Inside Left Solid Vocab
1. Crystalline: Solid with regular, ordered arrangement of particles.
2. Pressure: The action of pressing or pushing against something.
3. Freezing Point: Temperature at which a liquid becomes a solid.

Inside Left Gas Vocab
1. Compression: Force that squeezes something together.
2. Evaporation: To change from a liquid into a gas.
3. Sublimation: When a solid turns into a gas without first becoming a liquid.

Inside Right Liquid Vocab
1. Viscosity: A fluid's resistance to flow.
2. Melting Point: Temperature at which a solid becomes a liquid.
3. Condensation: To change from a gas to a liquid.

Inside Right Plasma Vocab
1. Ions: Atom or group of atoms that carries a positive or negative charge because of gaining or losing an electron.
2. Electrons: Negatively charged particle of an atom.
3. Northern Lights: Natural display of colored lights in the night sky.

Front

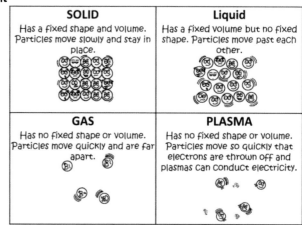

Inside Middle

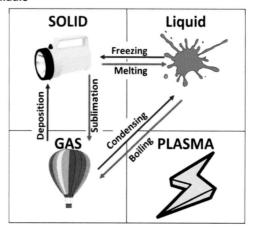

Matter and its States Quiz
1. B
2. D
3. B
4. C
5. D
6. A
7. D
8. A
9. A,B
10. G
11. A
12. D
13. C
14. I
15. F
16. A

→

Gas Laws
& Properties

40° Celsius   **25° Celsius**   **5° Celsius**

This week students will learn about three of the gas laws and how they work. Students will also learn the difference between a law and a theory.

Keywords:

Gas
Charles' Law

Gay-Lussac's Law
Boyle's Law

Scientific Law
Scientific Theory

Temperature
Volume

Day 1—Gas Law Notes + Ivory Soap Demo

Start off this unit with a cool demo showing how ivory soap expands dramatically in the microwave. Tell students that we will be learning the laws behind how gases behave. On this day students will learn about the different gas laws. You will find the presentation on our Resource page tinyurl.com/ybuwjcnx (password: Matter). You can download the PowerPoint file and give the presentation yourself (teaching tips are in the bottom notes of the PowerPoint). or you can use the recorded presentation. A student can watch the recorded presentation on their own to fill out their notes as they learn about three of the gas laws.

Day 2—Gas Law Challenge Labs

Using these fun mini labs students will see Boyle's Gas Law, Charles' Gas Law and Gay-Lussac's Gas Law in action. Have students fill out the gas law squares at the top of their lab sheet before beginning the lab.

We use station cards for these three mini gas law labs and include an optional extension activity on each card. Students can complete the extension activity at your direction or try them at home. We have also provided separate station cards for the extensions if you would like to include them as separate stations in your lab. To organize lab stations, we suggest having only 4 students (have students work in groups of two) at each station. Before beginning the lab make sure to tell students how they will rotate. Ex: If they start at Lab station 2 they will rotate to station 3 and then finish at 1.

Gay-Lussac's Mini Lab

Boyle's Mini Lab

Charles' Mini Lab

There are scientific laws that explain how gas behavior is connected to temperature, volume and pressure.

Day 3—Simulators and Syringes Online Labs

These two virtual labs will let students manipulate variables to see the different gas laws in action. The second virtual lab is a Phet simulation. Phet simulations are a fantastic free science resource. You or the student will need to <u>download it</u> onto a computer before being able to use the activity. As long as Adobe flash player and Java are installed all of these activities should work. You can try a different browser (google chrome, internet explorer or firefox) if you are having trouble. All of the sites are safe to visit and will not harm your computer. Co-op leaders and teachers, you can project these labs and work through them as a class. We like to have students take turns to complete each task while everyone fills out the handout together.

Materials:

- Goggles
- Food Coloring
- 60 ml Syringe (Amazon or Medical Supply Store)
- Casserole dish or plate with lip
- 2-Liter Bottle, empty
- Balloon
- Mini Marshmallows
- Tea Candle
- Bar of Ivory Soap
- Microwave

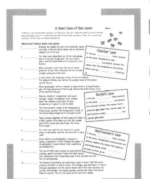

Day 4—A Real Case of Gas Laws

Using real life scenarios students will apply what they have learned about the gas laws to identify the gas law represented. They will need to read carefully and think about how pressure, temperature and volume are related in each situation. They can use their notes and lab sheet to assist them.

Day 5—QUIZ: Gas Laws and Properties

This is a culmination of the week's learning activities. This quiz will cover three of the gas laws and their rules and variables. Students should know the difference between a scientific law and theory. You can have students study their class work. They should pay special attention to the terms in bold. The vocabulary list in your guide can also help them to prepare. The student notebook does not have a copy of the quiz so you will want to make sure you have the quiz ready for them to take.

Next Generation Science Standards—Unit 3

MS-PS1-1: Matter of any type can be subdivided into particles that are too small to see, but even then the matter still exists and can be detected by other means. A model showing that gases are made from matter particles that are too small to see and are moving freely around in space can explain many observations, including the inflation and shape of a balloon and the effects of air on larger particles or objects.

MS-PS1-1: The term "heat" as used in everyday language refers both to thermal energy (the motion of atoms or molecules within a substance) and the transfer of that thermal energy from one object to another. In science, heat is used only for this second meaning; it refers to the energy transferred due to the temperature difference between two objects.

MS-PS1-4: The changes of state that occur with variations in temperature or pressure can be described and predicted using these models of matter.

Cross Cutting Concept-Cause and Effect (MS-PS1-4): Cause and effect relationships may be used to predict phenomena in natural or designed systems.

Exploding Ivory Soap Demo

Charles' Gas Law Demo

Materials:

- Bar of Ivory Soap
- Microwave
- Microwave safe plate

Caution: This experiment is safe to do in your microwave and will not make a mess. There will be a lingering smell of soap for about an hour after this demo. Do not heat soap in the microwave for longer than instructed.

Introduction:

When Ivory soap is made it is whipped to incorporate air, before it sets. This makes ivory soap bars so light that they float instead of sinking like other types of bar soaps.

What to Do:

1. Unwrap the bar of Ivory soap.
2. Put it on a plate and place it in the microwave.
3. Set the microwave for 2 minutes and watch as the soap dramatically expands.
4. Take out your plate of soap and let it cool for two minutes before touching it.
5. Allow students to lift the soap up and feel it.

What Happened:

Ivory soap expands almost seven times its size, almost filling an entire microwave! Ask students why they think this bar of soap expanded so much. If you need to, prompt students by reminding them that ivory soap is full of air (which is a gas). When the particles of a gas are heated up they move faster and take up more space. This is a perfect example of Charles' law, which states that as temperature increases the volume of a gas will also increase.

Gas Law Notes

Name:

Your teacher or parent will give you these notes or have you go to the resource page to watch the recorded presentation. Resource page: tinyurl.com/ybuwjcnx (password: Matter).

A Gas is one of the _____ states of matter. It has no _____ shape and no _____ volume. Its particles move so fast that they _____ and _____ around.

As _____ increases the _____ a _____ moves.

Charles' Law

As _____ increases _____ increases.

T ___ = V ___

From your experience or the slideshow, draw a picture example to illustrate this law.

Scientific Law

Is:

Example:

Scientific Theory

Is:

Example:

Gay-Lussac's Law

As _____ increases _____ increases.

T ___ = V ___

From your experience or the slideshow, draw a picture example to illustrate this law.

Boyle's Law

As _____ increases _____ decreases.

T ___ = V ___

From your experience or the slideshow, draw a picture example to illustrate this law.

What law does ivory soap and the microwave show?

Copyright © Easy Peasy Science Fair. All rights reserved.

36

3 Station Lab Cards—Mini Gas Labs

Cut up these station lab cards and place them at each station. Include materials for the extra activities if you would like for students to do them.

MARSHMALLOW SHRINKER (1)
BOYLE'S LAW

1. Put a mini marshmallow or two inside of your syringe and put the plunger down until it touches the top of your marshmallows.
2. Plug the tip of the syringe with its cap or by placing your finger on it.
3. Now pull the plunger up. What happens to your marshmallow?
4. Release your finger or the cap from the tip, pull the plunger to the top of the syringe.
5. Plug the tip of the syringe again and push the plunger down. What happens to your marshmallow?
6. Which variables were at play in this lab: Temperature, Pressure and/or Volume?
7. Explain how this is demonstrating Boyle's Law.

FUN EXTRA: Use your syringe to demonstrate how an increased or decreased pressure can change the boiling point of a liquid. Fill your syringe with about 20 mL of warm water. Remove the air from the syringe by pushing a little on the plunger. Plug the tip with your finger or a cap and pull the plunger up. Do you see the water start to boil? Can you explain why this happens using what you know about pressure and particle movement/energy?

*Note: this should be a 60 mL or 60 cc syringe or larger. You can get this at a drugstore or on Amazon. You can also do this lab with a small balloon, partially filled, instead of a marshmallow.

A BUNCH OF HOT AIR (2)
CHARLES' LAW

1. Take an empty, 2-liter bottle or a gallon milk jug and put a party balloon on top of it.
2. Place your bottle in a bowl or casserole dish full of hot water, an adult can pour this for you. What happens to your balloon?
3. Now, place your bottle in a bowl or casserole dish full of ice water. What happens to your balloon?
4. Which variables were at play in this lab: Temperature, Pressure and/or Volume?
5. Explain how this is demonstrating Charles' Law.

FUN EXTRA: A quick Charles' law experiment is to dent a ping pong ball and to then use a hair dryer on it. What happens?
If you used a 2-liter bottle for this lab, try making a Cartesian diver this shows **BOYLE'S LAW**, in action. Fill your bottle up with water. Put a ketchup or soy sauce packet in it (these have air trapped inside so they will float in the bottle). You can also trap air in a drinking straw by folding it and closing the ends with a paper clip. Screw the lid onto your bottle and squeeze the sides. What happens to the "diver" inside? Use what you know about Boyle's law to describe why you think this is happening.

*Note: a larger bottle holds more air and is better than a smaller bottle so we suggest a 2-liter or gallon bottle.

3 Station Lab Cards—Mini Gas Labs

Cut up these station lab cards and place them at each station. Include materials for the extra activities if you would like for students to do them.

CANDLE VACUUM (3)
GAY-LUSSAC'S LAW

SAFETY: An adult should be present. Wear your safety goggles.
1. Put water into a casserole dish or onto a plate, about ¼ inch high. If you have food coloring put 3–4 drops of a color into the water.
2. Place a tea candle in the middle of the casserole dish.
3. Light the candle and place a clear cup or jar over the candle.
4. Watch as the candle goes out. What do you see happen to the water?
5. Repeat this experiment at least one more time, now that you know what you are looking at.
6. Which variables were at play in this lab: Temperature, Pressure and/or Volume?
7. Explain how this is demonstrating Gay-Lussac's Law.

FUN EXTRA: With adult supervision, put about a tablespoon of water in a clean soda can. Place this can on a hotplate or the burner of your stove. When you see steam coming out of the can, use tongs to pick up the can and place it upside down into a bowl of ice water. What happened? Use what you know about Gay-Lussac's law to describe why you think this happened.

*Note: If you do not have a tea candle you can use a votive or any candle that will fit under your jar or cup.

Use these 6 station lab cards if you would like to turn the extra activities into separate lab stations. Cut up these station lab cards and place them at each station.

MARSHMALLOW SHRINKER (1)
BOYLE'S LAW

1. Put a mini marshmallow or two inside of your syringe and put the plunger down until it touches the top of your marshmallows.
2. Plug the tip of the syringe with its cap or by placing your finger on it.
3. Now pull the plunger up. What happens to your marshmallow?
4. Release your finger or the cap from the tip, pull the plunger to the top of the syringe.
5. Plug the tip of the syringe again and push the plunger down. What happens to your marshmallow?
6. Which variables were at play in this lab: Temperature, Pressure and/or Volume?
7. Explain how this is demonstrating Boyle's Law.

*Note: this should be a 60 mL or 60 cc syringe or larger. You can get this at a drugstore or on Amazon. You can also do this lab with a small balloon, partially filled, instead of a marshmallow.

A BUNCH OF HOT AIR (2)
CHARLES' LAW

1. Take an empty, 2-liter bottle or a gallon milk jug and put a party balloon on top of it.
2. Place your bottle in a bowl or casserole dish full of hot water, an adult can pour this for you. What happens to your balloon?
3. Now, place your bottle in a bowl or casserole dish full of ice water. What happens to your balloon?
4. Which variables were at play in this lab: Temperature, Pressure and/or Volume?
5. Explain how this is demonstrating Charles' Law.

*Note: a larger bottle holds more air and is better than a smaller bottle so we suggest a 2-liter or gallon bottle.

6 Station Lab Cards—Mini Gas Labs

Use these 6 station lab cards if you would like to turn the extra activities into separate lab stations. Cut up these station lab cards and place them at each station.

CANDLE VACUUM (3)
GAY-LUSSAC'S LAW

1. An adult should be present. Wear your safety goggles.
2. Put water into a casserole dish or onto a plate, about ¼ inch h[igh]. [If you] have food coloring put 3–4 drops of a color into the water.
3. Place a tea candle in the middle of the casserole dish.
4. Light the candle and place a clear cup or jar over the candle.
5. Watch as the candle goes out. What do you see happen to the water?
6. Repeat this experiment at least one more time, now that you know what you are looking at.
7. Which variables were at play in this lab: Temperature, Pressure and/or Volume?
8. Explain how this is demonstrating Gay-Lussac's Law.

*Note: If you do not have a tea candle you can use a votive or any candle that will fit under your jar or cup.

ANOTHER WAY TO BOIL WATER (4)
PRESSURE AND BOILING POINT

1. Fill your syringe with about 20 mL of warm water.
2. Remove the air from the syringe by pushing a little on the plunger.
3. Plug the tip of the syringe with its cap or by placing your finger on it.
4. Pull up on the plunger.
5. Do you see the water start to boil? Can you explain why this happens using what you know about pressure and particle movement/energy?

Use these 6 station lab cards if you would like to turn the extra activities into separate lab stations. Cut up these station lab cards and place them at each station.

CARTESIAN DIVER (5)
BOYLE'S LAW

1. Fill your 2-liter bottle up with water.

2. Put your diver in: This needs to be something with air in it: Soy sauce packet, capped dropper, ketchup packet or a folded drinking straw with a paper clip to close the ends.

3. Your diver should be floating, if it sinks to the bottom try a different diver.

4. Screw the lid of your bottle closed and squeeze your bottle. What happens to your diver?

5. Which variables were at play in this lab: Temperature, Pressure and/or Volume?

6. Explain how this is demonstrating Boyle's Law.

*Note: this can be done with a smaller bottle.

CRUSHED CAN (6)
GAY-LUSSAC'S LAW

SAFETY: An adult should be present. Wear your safety goggles and use caution around heat sources.

1. Put a tablespoon of water into an empty, clean soda can.

2. Use tongs to pick up the can and place it on a hotplate or the burner of your stove (the adult can do this)

3. When you see steam coming out of the can, use tongs to pick up the can and place it upside down into a bowl of ice water. What happens?

4. Which variables were at play in this lab: Temperature, Pressure and/or Volume?

5. Explain how this is demonstrating Gay-Lussac's Law.

GAS LAW CHALLENGE LABS

Name: _____

Fill out the squares below from what you have already learned. Fill out the rest of this worksheet as you visit each station.

BOYLE'S LAW

Pressure and _____ are inversely related. This means that if pressure goes ↓ then volume goes ↑. If pressure goes _____ then volume goes ↓.

CHARLES' LAW

_____ and volume are directly related. This means that temperature and volume either both go ↓ or both go _____.

GAY-LUSSAC'S LAW

Temperature and pressure are directly related;. This means that the pressure and temperature either _____ go ↓ or both go ↑.

MARSHMALLOW SHRINKER - BOYLE'S LAW

1. What happened to the marshmallows when you pulled the plunger up?

2. What happened to the marshmallows when you pushed the plunger down?

3. Circle the variables that were at play in this lab:

   Temperature   **Volume**   **Pressure**

4. How did this lab demonstrate Boyle's Law?

Boiling Water Extra: Why is the water boiling in your syringe?

A BUNCH OF HOT AIR- CHARLES' LAW

Safety: Wear your Goggles, Do this with Adult Supervision

1. What happens to the balloon in the hot water?

2. What happens to the balloon in the cold water?

3. Circle the variables that were at play in this lab:

   Temperature   **Volume**   **Pressure**

Charles' Lab Continued:

4. How did this lab demonstrate Charles' Law?

Ping Pong Extra: What happens to the ping pong ball? Why?

BOYLE'S LAW – Cartesian Diver Extra: What happened to your diver? Using what you know about Boyle's law describe why you think this happened.

CANDLE VACUUM- GAY-LUSSAC'S LAW

Safety: Wear your Goggles.
Do this with Adult Supervision.

1. Draw a picture showing what happened to the water as the candle went out?

2. Circle the variables that were at play in this lab:

   Temperature   **Volume**   **Pressure**

3. How did this lab demonstrate Gay-Lussac's Law?

Crushing Can Extra: What happened to the can? Use what you know about Gay Lussac's Law to describe why this happened.

Simulators and Syringes

Name:

There are so many fantastic free activities and interactive labs online. Answer the questions on this sheet as you explore these activities and online labs.

Interactive Syringe

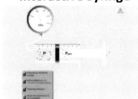

Go to: tinyurl.com/bxu4eea

Click Enter and then check all but the bottom box so that you can see the inside and outside air.

1. Can you push the piston of the syringe all the way to zero? Why or why not?

2. How do you make the pressure higher (hPa: hectopascal is the SI unit for measuring pressure)? What is the highest you can get it to go?

3. How do you make the pressure lower? What is the lowest the pressure will go?

4. So when the Volume of the air in the syringe decreases, the molecules get _____ together and the _____ increases. What law does this represent?

Phet: Gas Particle Simulator

Go to: tinyurl.com/muun3xg

Click **Download** and open the download. Note, you will need flash installed in order to use this simulation.

1. Take a few minutes to play around with this simulation. Can you change the pressure, temperature and number of molecules in your tank?

2. Can you blow the lid off the container just by changing the mass (amount of gas molecules) in the container?

3. Hit reset and pump air 3 or 4 times into the container. What happens to the particles when you add or remove heat to the container?

4. Describe how changing the volume affects pressure and temperature in this simulation.

5. Describe how changing the temperature affects pressure and volume in this simulation.

6. Make the temperature constant (stay the same) by selecting it in the upper left. How are pressure and volume related in this simulation?

7. Fill in the table below. Hit reset before you begin working on a new law. Don't forget you can freeze or make each item constant on the left side.

	Charles' Law	Gay-Lussac's Law	Boyle's Law
How did you demonstrate this in the simulation?			
Volume: decrease/ increase			
Temperature			
Pressure Atm			

8. Use the simulator to solve this question:

   You check the pressure of your bike's tires on a very cold day and find that they are 30 psi (psi = pounds per square inch. It is another way to measure pressure). You filled your tires just the day before It was very warm that day. Assuming there is no leak in your tires, what would explain this change in pressure? What law is this?

A Real Case of Gas Laws

Name:

Different scientists helped to develop our Gas Laws. Use your notes and what you have learned about each gas law to fill in the blanks for each of the three laws below. Then tell us which law matches with the real world examples below.

Which Law? Charles, Boyle, Gay-Lussac:

1. _____ Pushing the nozzle of a can of air freshener opens up a hole in the can which allows the air freshener expand out of the can.

2. _____ You take your basketball out of the cold garage and it is too flat to play with. The next day is warm and the basketball is at full pressure and bouncy.

3. _____ When you open a hot oven the hot air inside puffs out at you. This is because the air is under a higher pressure in the oven.

4. _____ A torch heats the molecules inside of a hot air balloon. The balloon inflates and carries the people inside of the basket up into the air.

5. _____ When gunpowder burns, it creates a large amount of superheated gas. The high pressure of the hot gas behind the bullet forces it out of the barrel of the gun.

6. _____ Placing a balloon in extremely cold liquid nitrogen makes the balloon much smaller. When the balloon is put back at room temperature it gains its volume back.

7. _____ The thermometer inside of the Thanksgiving turkey pops up when the temperature inside of the bird is high enough for it to be safe to eat.

8. _____ Twist a straw together on both sides until there is a tight pocket of air. When you flick this middle part of the straw with your finger, the straw bursts open.

9. _____ Put a hot can, with hot air inside of it, upside down in cold water and the can will crush in upon itself.

10. _____ Since there is no atmospheric pressure in space, a spacesuit is vital. It keeps the gases in an astronaut's blood stream from expanding and killing them.

11. _____ The can of PAM I use to spray my pans before cooking, says to not get it close to a heat source. This is because if the compressed gas in this can gets too hot, the can will explode.

12. _____ The bends is something all scuba divers want to avoid. With the extra pressure of water on top of a diver, the nitrogen gas decreases in volume and gets absorbed into the diver's blood cells. If the diver ascends too quickly, the nitrogen will rapidly expand, causing the cells in the diver's body to rupture. This can be super painful and even deadly.

Charles' Law

In this law _____ stays constant or the same. Temperature and _____ are directly related. This means that the temperature and volume either both go _____ or both go up.

Boyle's Law

In this law _____ stays constant or the same. _____ and Volume are inversely related. This means that if pressure goes down then volume goes up, and if pressure goes _____ then volume goes down.

Gay-Lussac's Law

In this law _____ or the same. Temperature and pressure are directly related. This means that pressure and temperature either _____ go down or both go up.

40° Celsius 25° Celsius 5° Celsius

Name:

Gas Laws and Properties Quiz

Multiple Choice

Identify the choice that best completes the statement or answers the question.

_____ 1. Maggie made a poster to compare scientific laws and scientific theories. Which of the following statements should Maggie include on her poster to summarize the difference between scientific laws and scientific theories?

a. Scientific laws are frequently modified, but scientific theories are rarely changed as new information becomes available.

c. Scientific theories explain why something happens, and scientific laws describe what happens.

b. Scientific laws and theories are actually the same. Maggie should get an "F" on her project.

d. Scientific theories are based on observation, and scientific laws are based on opinions.

_____ 2. Which best describes a scientific theory?

a. The conclusion a scientist comes to after an experiment.

c. The opinion of a scientist.

b. a well-supported and widely accepted explanation of why something in nature happens..

d. a statement that describes an observable occurrence in nature that is always be true.

_____ 3. Increased gas pressure can be caused by _____.

a. Gas molecules hitting other gas molecules.

c. Gas molecules hitting the walls of containers.

b. Gas molecules reacting with other gas molecules.

d. Gas molecules heating up.

_____ 4. Which gas law do the balloons at the top of the page illustrate?

a. That gas particles get larger at higher temperatures.

c. Amount of gas particles increases at high temperatures.

b. Gas particles move more slowly and get closer together at higher temperatures.

d. Gas particles move faster and farther apart at higher temperatures.

_____ 5. What happens to gas particles when they are cold?

a. Nothing.

c. They usually slow down and become a solid.

b. They usually speed up and become Plasma.

d. They usually slow down and become a liquid.

_____ 6. There are only 2 states of matter which CAN be compressed. These are _____ and _____.

a. Gas, Plasma

c. Liquid, Gas

b. Solid, Liquid

d. Plasma, Liquid

Matching

Match the law to the examples and descriptions that it applies to.

a. Gay-Lussac's Law   b. Boyle's Law   c. Charles' Law

_____ 7. Which law explains why there are more car accidents from bursting tires in hot weather?

_____ 8. Gary dented his ping pong ball but was able to get it back to its original round shape by blasting it with warm air from a hair dryer. What law is this an example of?

_____ 9. If temperature is increased then pressure will also increase (as long as the volume remains the same).

_____ 10. When gunpowder burns, it creates a large amount of superheated gas. The high pressure of the hot gas behind the bullet forces it out of the barrel of the gun.

_____ 11. Emily sat down on a balloon causing it to pop.

_____ 12. As temperature increases the volume will also increase (as long as the pressure remains the same).

_____ 13. When you block the top of a syringe with marshmallows in it, the marshmallow will get bigger when you pull on the syringe. The marshmallows will shrink when you push the syringe in.

_____ 14. When the pressure increases, the volume decreases (as long as the temperature remains the same).

_____ 15. When I put Ivory soap in the microwave, the soap expanded into a big fluffy ball that was at least 10 times the size of the original bar of soap.

Gas Law Notes
Four; fixed; fixed; separate; fly
Temperature; faster; particle
<u>Charles' Law</u>: Temperature; Volume T↑=V↑
<u>Picture</u>: Egg in a bottle
<u>Scientific Law</u>: Fact or rule that describes the behavior of something in nature. Example: Planets orbit the sun
<u>Scientific Theory</u>: Explains why a law happens. Can be disproved and changed. Example: planets orbit the sun <u>because</u> the sun's gravity pulls on them.
<u>Gay-Lussac's Law</u>: Temperature; Pressure; T↑=P↑
<u>Picture</u>: Can of soda on hot day.
<u>Boyle's Law</u>: Pressure; Volume ; P↑=V↓
<u>Picture</u>: Cartesian Diver
Ivory Soap in the microwave is an example of Charles' Law. As the temperature increases the gas particles in the soap expand making the soap inflate.
<u>**Variables:**</u>
<u>Independent Variable</u>: should be the variable being tested. Example: right leg used to kick
<u>Dependent Variable</u>: is the result, the variable being measured. Example: how far the ball was kicked
<u>Control Group</u>: This group is used to compare. It makes sure that the independent variable is tested

Gas Law Challenge Labs
<u>Boyle's Law</u>: Volume; Up↑

<u>Charles' Law</u>: Temperature; Up↑

<u>Gay-Lussac's Law</u>: Both

<u>Marshmallow Shrinker-Boyle's Law:</u>
1. Your marshmallow or balloon should get bigger.
2. Your marshmallow or balloon should shrink.
3. Pressure and Volume
4. When the plunger pushes down on the air in the syringe it is pushing the air particles closer together causing the pressure to be higher and the marshmallow to be smaller. Boyle's law states that as pressure increases the volume decreases.
Extra: When you pull the plunger out there you lower the air pressure in the syringe. Since there is less pressure pushing the particles together they can move fast enough to vaporize (turn to a gas) even at a lower temperature. Boiling happens when particles are vaporizing.

<u>A Bunch of Hot Air-Charles' Law:</u>
1. Your marshmallow or balloon should get bigger.
2. The balloon should inflate quickly.
3. The balloon will slightly deflate right away. Leave it in the cold and it will continue to deflate.
4. Temperature and Volume
5. When the bottle of air was placed in the hot water the temperature of the air in the bottle rose and the balloon inflated. In the ice bath the temp fell and the volume of the balloon did too. Charles' law states that as the temperature goes up the volume goes up.
Cartesian Diver Extra: The diver sinks when you push on the bottle. This is because by squeezing the bottle the air particles in your diver also get pushing closer together and denser. They become denser than the water in the bottle causing your diver to sink.
Ping Pong Extra: When the hair dryer warms the air in the dented ping pong ball, the volume of the air expands causing the ball to become round again.

<u>Candle Vacuum- Law:</u>
1. Should show the water in the cup rising higher than the water in the dish.
2. Temperature and Pressure
3. The heat from the flame causes the air in the container to expand and some gets pushed out of the container and into the water. When the flame goes out, the lower temperature causes the air particles to contract (get smaller) and the air pressure becomes lower than the air pressure outside of the container. The higher outside air pressure is pushing down on the water. This causes the outside air pressure to push water into the container until the pressure is equal.
→

Extra: The hot air in the can contracts (gets smaller) when the can is plunged in ice water. When the air contracts the air pressure inside the can is not as strong as the air pressure outside of the can. The hole in the can is also too small to let enough water in quickly enough to equalize the air pressure. The stronger air pressure outside of the can then crushes the can.

Simulators and Syringes
<u>Interactive Syringe:</u>
1. No, the gas particles can be compressed a lot but not completely since they are matter and still take up space.
2. You push the syringe in. This forces the particles together making the pressure higher.
3. Pull the syringe out. This gives the particles more room to move making the pressure lower.
4. Closer; pressure. Boyle's Law

<u>PHET Online Gas Particles Simulator:</u>
1. Yes.
2. Yes.
3. Move faster when I add heat and slower when I remove it.
4. As the pressure gets higher the temperature is also getting higher. Also when I add heat I can make the pressure high enough to blow the lid off of the container.
5. When the volume increases the temperature and the pressure go down. When the volume decreases then both of them go up.
6. As the volume of the container decreases the pressure increases.

	Charles Law	Gay-Lussac's Law	Boyle's Law
How did you demonstrate this in the simulation?	Made Pressure Constant. Added heat and as temp went up volume increased.	Made Volume Constant. Added heat = pressure and temp went up	Made Temp Constant. Increased Volume and pressure decreased.
Volume:	Increase	Same/Constant	Increase
Temperature	558 K (will vary)	547 K (will vary)	547 K (will vary)
Pressure Atm	1.62 (will vary)	1.88 (will vary)	1.70 (will vary)

8. On a cold day the particles would not be moving as much and would be closer together. Because of this the particles would have less pressure in the tires would be lower. Gay-Lussac's Law

A Real Case of Gas Laws
Charles Law: Pressure; Volume; down
Boyle's Law: Temperature; Pressure; up
Gay-Lussac's Law: Volume; both
1. Boyle
2. Charles
3. Gay-Lussac
4. Charles
5. Gay-Lussac
6. Charles
7. Charles
8. Boyle
9. Gay-Lussac
10. Boyle
11. Gay-Lussac
12. Boyle

Scientific Method and Safety Quiz
1. C
2. B
3. D
4. D
5. D
6. A
7. A
8. C
9. A
10. A
11. B
12. C
13. B
14. B
15. C

Mixtures & Solutions

Mixtures & Solutions

This week students will learn about mixtures and solutions and how these are not chemical reactions but just a physical change.

Keywords:

Solvent
Solute
Solubility
Saturation

Universal Solvent
Aqueous Solution
Viscosity
Clarity

Homogenous Mixture
Heterogenous Mixture
Alloy
Atom

Molecule
Compound
Element

Day 1—Solution to a Great Mix Up! (Movie Notes)

Using these fun short videos students will be introduced to what solvents and solutes are and to the difference between mixtures and solutions. Students will watch the video links, answering questions along the way. There are 37 total minutes of video to watch. Co-op leaders and teachers, you can use a projector to show these videos to the entire class. You might need to repeat a video or slow it down by going to settings ✿ and adjusting the speed to 0.75 so that students get all the information in these videos.

Day 2—Fake Blood Lab

We know this is a gross and messy lab but this is an Ooey Gooey Chemistry book so you should expect a little gross and messy! In this lab students will make stage blood, which is a solution. This stuff will stain, so students should dress appropriately and work in an area that can get messy. As students mix more and more ingredients (solutes) into the solvent (water) they are looking at different properties of matter such as clarity and viscosity. Our favorite part is step 2; it is really surprising to see how all of the powdered sugar dissolves in the small amount of water. It is even more surprising that the water does not rise that much. This is because the small sugar molecules fit in the spaces between the larger water molecules.

Making edible barf (yes, gross) is the extension to this lab. It is easy to make this mixture (not a solution) and it looks like the real thing. We have included a video of Nasa scientists making simulated vomit to test the barf bags in the space shuttle. Watching this video before the lab might be a good intro and give you a chance to talk about how the scientists in this video are using good lab techniques, such as wafting with their hands instead of directly smelling a container.

!Big !idea

Many of the liquids, gases and solids that make up our world are mixtures. Mixtures have properties you can observe.

Day 3—Great Ways to Get Together T-Chart

Learning note taking strategies while reading multiple articles is an important skill for students to learn. In this lesson students read an article on mixtures and an article on solutions. They should include all of the guideline prompts in their T-chart. Several of the quiz questions are taken directly from these articles, so encourage students to be thorough and to get the best information they can.

Day 4—Atom, Molecule or Mixture?

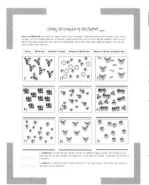

Using crazy faced atoms, students will learn the difference between atoms of an element and molecules. Molecules are when two or more atoms (even the same type of atoms) are joined together. A mixture has two or more different atoms or molecules mixed together. This is a good exercise and students will become more aware of molecules and atoms. They will apply what they have learned about mixtures to identify mixtures of atoms and molecules.

Two Types of Atoms:
Mixture of Atoms

Three of the same atoms joined together:
A Molecule

Two different types of atoms joined together:
A Molecule

Two Types of Molecules:
Mixture of Molecules

Day 5—QUIZ: Matter and its States

This is a culmination of the week's learning activities. You can have students study their class work. They should pay special attention to the terms in bold. The information from the T-chart plays a big role in the quiz. The quiz will cover different types of mixtures and solutions and the terms that apply to them. The vocabulary list in your guide can also help them to prepare. The student notebook does not have a copy of the quiz so you will want to make sure you have the quiz ready for them to take.

Next Generation Science Standards—Unit 4

MS-PS1-1: Develop models to describe the atomic composition of simple molecules and extended structures.

MS-PS1-1a: Substances are made from different types of atoms, which combine with one another in various ways. Atoms form molecules that range in size from two to thousands of atoms.

MS-PS1-2: Analyze and interpret data on the properties of substances before and after the substances interact to determine if a chemical reaction has occurred.

MS-PS1-4: Gases and liquids are made of molecules or inert atoms that are moving about relative to each other.

Solution to a Great Mix Up!

Name:

There are many fantastic free learning videos on the internet. Answer the questions on this sheet as you watch the following videos. You might need to rewatch these short videos once or twice to answer the questions.

The Great Picnic Mix Up: Crash Course Kids (4:10)

Go to: tinyurl.com/q8h2osx

If this is too fast, you can slow down the video. Go to settings ⚙ > Speed> 0.75

1. Anytime you combine _____ or more different things you get a _____.

2. Circle the solution:
   Sand and Water   Sugar and Water

3. The SOLVENT is ____ and the SOLUTE is ____.
   a. The part of the solution that is dissolved
   b. The part which does the dissolving

4. What is solubility?

5. What is saturation?

7. Put and **M** next to the mixture and an **S** next to the solution at the picnic.

   Iced Tea _____   Fruit Salad _____

Mixtures and Solutions: Brainstew (23:14)

Go to: tinyurl.com/p3ez3wa

1. Into what two groups can we divide the states of matter?

2. What happens if you let salad dressing sit for a while?

3. Why is her breakfast cereal a mixture?

4. Why is the powdered drink she makes a solution?

5. All _____ are _____ but not all _____ are _____.

6. How did they separate the mixture of charcoal and water in the lab?

7. What are the two white solutions they test against each other? Which one wasn't a mixture and how do you know?

8. As they add sugar and vanilla to milk and cream, they are turning it into ice cream. Ice Cream is a _____.

9. How many times a day do they have to milk a cow?

10. Milk right out of a cow is a _____. Milk from the store is a _____.

Dirty Laundry Crash Course (stop at 7:00)

Go to: tinyurl.com/km6258d

This talks about the universal solvent (water). This is a little advanced, but he is fun to listen to. For students who want to know more, it is a great episode!

1. Without water, none of the _____ _____ that keep you alive would happen.

2. Why is water the key?

3. Why is bleach so good at its job?

4. Hydrogen peroxide is a _____. Water is the _____ and hydrogen peroxide the _____.

5. Why is water such a good solvent?
   a. There is a lot of it.
   b. It is _____
   c. It is _____

6. A water based solution is an _____ solution.

7. What is something that water does not dissolve?

Fake Blood Lab

Name:

We are going to make edible stage blood as we learn about solutions, solutes, solvents, viscosity and saturation!

Lab Safety | **Aprons on!**
This can be a messy lab so dress appropriately. This is a good lab to do outside or in an area that can be easily cleaned up.

Background Info:

- In this lab, you will dissolve solutes like sugar, corn starch and cocoa powder into a solvent (water). Water is considered the universal solvent because it is a liquid at a wide range of temperatures and it can dissolve so many different things.
- We are adding 4 times the amount of powdered sugar to our solvent than we have water. In doing this we are creating a thick super saturated solution.

Materials:

Water	Ziploc Bag	Corn Starch	Red Food Coloring	Clear Cup (greater than ½ cup capacity)
Teaspoon	Spoon	¼ Measuring Cup	Cocoa Powder	1 Cup Powdered Sugar

Procedure:

1. Measure ¼ cup of water into your cup. This water is your solvent, observe its **viscosity** (flow/thickness) and **clarity** (clearness).

2. You have four times the amount of solute (sugar) as you do solvent (water). Do you think that the entire cup of powdered sugar will dissolve in this water? Mark on the cup how high you think your solution will rise, in the cup, once you have mixed all the solute and solvent.

3. Use your spoon to slowly sift powdered sugar into your cup, occasionally stirring the solution with the spoon. Is the water still clear? Has the viscosity changed?

4. Pour your sugar/water solution into your baggy. Make sure to firmly seal the top. Use your fingers to finish mixing this solution through the bag.

5. Add 25 drops of red food coloring. Has this affected the clarity or viscosity of your solutions?

6. Add a teaspoon of cocoa powder. When something dissolves easily in water it has a **high solubility**. Comparing this cocoa powder to the powdered sugar, which had a higher solubility?

7. In your cup mix 1 teaspoon of water with 2 teaspoons of corn starch until this mixture is smooth and free of lumps. Now add this cornstarch mixture to your bag.

8. Observe your fake blood. Would you say that it is a solution or a mixture? Why? How has the viscosity and clarity changed since you started out with just water?

Data Tables:

Qualitative Data:

These solutes are made of different molecules and interact with water in their own unique ways. List the similarities and differences between how these solutes mixed with the solvent (water).

Cocoa	Sugar	Cornstarch

Questions:

1. In your own words describe:
    a. Solute:

    b. Solvent:

    c. Solution:

2. List 2 things from the real world with a high viscosity and two things with a low viscosity.

3. Were you surprised about how much sugar you were able to dissolve into your water and at how little the water rose? Use the pictures to help you explain why adding ¼ cup water with 1 cup sugar did not equal 1 ¼ cups of solution.

Water Molecules   Water and Sugar Molecules

Fun Extra: Edible Barf Mixture

Nasa chemists actually simulate the texture and smell of real vomit to test their barf bags. We are just going to make a mixture that LOOKS like vomit. Check out this video if you want to see real Nasa chemists working in their lab to make simulated (fake) vomit! tinyurl.com/ydy49zms

To make realistic looking but edible barf follow this recipe. Why is this a mixture and not a solution?

1 pkg unflavored gelatin	¼ cup applesauce	yellow food coloring	¼ tsp cocoa powder
¼ cup oatmeal	¼ cup raisin bran cereal	microwavable bowl or mixing cup	

1. Heat the applesauce in the microwave for 1 minute. This will be hot so be careful and have an adult present.
2. Stir in 1 packet of unflavored gelatin for 1 minute.
3. Add 2 drops of yellow food coloring and the cocoa powder. Mix thoroughly.
4. Mix the oatmeal and raisin bran together. Add half of it into your applesauce mixture and stir very gently just to mix.
5. Spread this barf mixture onto a plate so that it resembles vomit, adding extra raisins or cereal pieces as desired.
6. Allow the barf to cool completely (a couple of hours). Remove it from the plate with a spatula.
7. Have fun!

Great Ways to Get Together

T-Chart

A T-Chart is used to compare two different concepts or things. Today you are going to make a T-Chart comparing Mixtures and Solutions as you read an online article by Chem4Kids: tinyurl.com/4mndk5p .

There are four short pages to read in this article: Mixture I, Mixture II, Solutions I and Solutions II. As you read, make your T-Chart on another sheet of paper, following these guidelines.

Mixtures	Solutions
• Define what a Mixture is.	• Define what a Solution is.
• Does a chemical or physical change occur?	• Does a chemical or physical change occur?
• Heterogenous and/or Homogenous? Why?	• Heterogenous and/or Homogenous? Why?
• Fact/Difference	• Fact/Difference
• Fact/Difference	• Fact/Difference
• Examples	• Examples
• Picture	• Picture

Mixtures and Solutions T-Chart

Name:

Mixtures	Solutions

Atom, Molecule or Mixture? Name:

Atoms and Molecules are words you need to know if you are going to deal with mixtures and chemistry. Each atom is the basic unit of a chemical element. A molecule is when two or more different or the same types of atoms, chemically join together. See if you can identify the atoms, molecules, and mixtures of them below. Write the correct label under each square. You will use some of them more than once.

Atoms	Molecules	Mixture of Atoms	Mixture of Molecules	Mixture of Atoms and Molecules

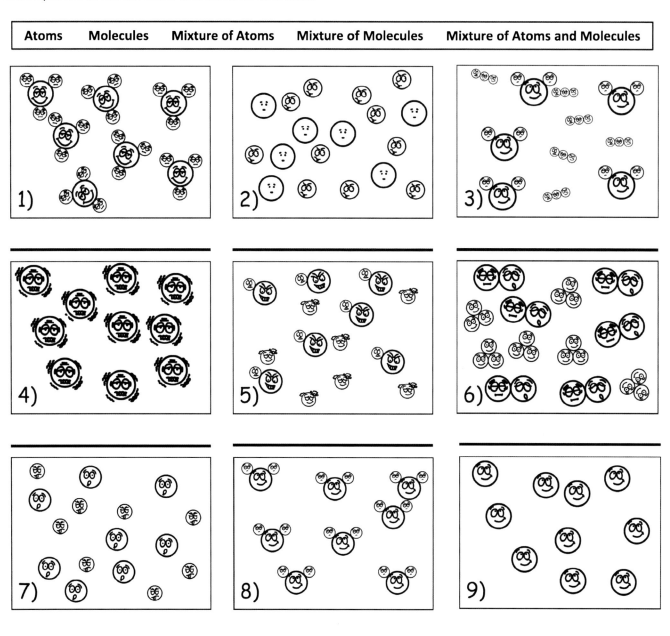

10) A **compound** is a molecule that contains at least two different types of atoms. All compounds are molecules but not all molecules are compounds. Write down the number of each box that contains a compound.

_____

11) An **element** is a substance that is made entirely from one type of atom. Write down the number of the boxes that are elements.

_____

Mixtures and Solutions Quiz

Multiple Choice

Identify the choice that best completes the statement or answers the question.

_____ 1. Which of these is an example of a heterogenous mixture?

    a. sand and water   b. fake blood   c. cake batter   d. sugar and water

_____ 2. The substance that dissolves another to make a solution is called a _____.

    a. solvent.   b. saturation   c. solute   d. suspension

_____ 3. A mixture of two or more metals is known as a(an) _____.

    a. carat   b. pure metal   c. alloy   d. girder

_____ 4. Which of these is a solution and not just a mixture?

    a. carbonated soda   b. salt water   c. milk   d. all of the above

_____ 5. The most common solvent on Earth, also known as the universal solvent is _____.

    a. turpentine   b. gasoline   c. water   d. alcohol

_____ 6. Distilled water only has water molecules in it. This would be an example of a _____.

    a. Solution   b. Homogenous Mixture   c. Mixture   d. Pure substance

_____ 7. Which liquid has the best clarity?

    a. water   b. syrup   c. coffee   d. milk

_____ 8. Mandy added so much sugar to her tea that no more sugar could be dissolved in it. Her tea was what type of solution?

    a. concentrated   b. dilution   c. saturated   d. solvent

_____ 9. Which of the following liquids has the highest viscosity?

    a. water   b. rubbing alcohol   c. apple juice   d. ketchup

_____ 10. Which of the following is an example of a mixture?

    a. food coloring and water   b. lemonade   c. fruit salad   d. all of the above

_____ 11. Vanilla dissolves better in alcohol than water. Alcohol dissolves vanilla to make vanilla extract, which can be used to flavor things like cakes and cookies. When vanilla extract is made, vanilla is the _____.

    a. suspension   b. solute   c. saturation   d. solvent

Matching

Match one or more of the choices that best complete the statement or answer the question.

    a. Atoms   b. Molecules   c. Mixture of Atoms

    d. Mixture of Molecules   e. Mixture of Atoms and Molecules

_____ 12.   _____ 13.   _____ 14.   _____ 15.

Answer Key—Unit 4: Mixtures & Solutions

Solutions to a Great Mix Up!
1: The Great Picnic Mix Up: Crash Course Kids
1. Two; Mixture
2. Sugar and Water
3. Solvent: B   Solute: A
4. The measure of a substance's ability to be dissolved
5. The point at which no more solute can dissolve in a solution.
6. Iced Tea: S   Fruit Salad: M

2: Mixtures and Solutions: Brainstew
1. Mixtures and Solutions
2. It separates
3. It is a mix of different foods and you can easily separate it.
4. It dissolves or spreads evenly throughout.
5. All <u>solutions</u> are <u>mixtures</u> but not all <u>mixtures</u> are <u>solutions</u>.
6. They used filter paper.
7. Celite and water; milk. Milk wasn't a mixture because it did not filter apart.
8. Solution
9. Twice
10. Mixture;Solution

3: Dirty Laundry Crash Course
1. Chemical reactions
2. It is really good at dissolving stuff.
3. It is a strong oxidizer.
4. Solution; solvent; solute
5. B: liquid at a lot of temperatures.
   C: It is polar and is really good at dissolving polar things
6. Aqueous
7. Oil

Fake Blood Lab (Sample Answers)
1. The water has a low viscosity because it flows really easily. It has good clarity, I can see right through it.
2. Answers will vary, but students should hypothesize how high the sugar and water will rise when combined.
3. The water now seems cloudy, I can see light through it though. It is definitely thicker so I would say it has a higher viscosity.
5. The viscosity is the same. I would say that the clarity was affected a little.
6. The powdered sugar dissolved more easily, it has a higher solubility.
8. This is a solution, not a mixture. Everything is mixed evely throughout. The viscosity is much higher than when we started. The powdered sugar and the corn starch affected the viscosity the most. The clarity has changed a lot too. I can now not see through the bag at all. The powdered sugar, corn starch and cocoa powder affected the clarity the most.

Data Table:
Cocoa: Did not have a high solubility, affected the clarity.
Sugar: Easily mixed —had a high solubility, did not raise the volume of the water much.
Cornstarch: Did not mix well (low solubility), clumps easily, affected the viscosity and clarity

Questions:
1.   a) Solute: What is dissolved into the solvent.
      b) Solvent: dissolves the solutes
      c) Solution: A mixture where the ingredients are evely spread throughout.
2. Answers will vary. Sample answers: High Viscosity: Syrup, honey   Low Viscosity: Juice, Vinegar
3. From the picture, I can see that there are spaces between the water molecules. The sugar molecules are smaller and fit into these spaces. This is why the water did not raise that much.

Mixtures	Solutions
Define what a Mixture is. **Anything you can combine is a mixture.**	Define what a Solution is. **A solution is a type of mixture but all of the molecules are evenly spread throughout the system. These are also called homogenous mixtures.**
Does a chemical or physical change occur? **In a Mixture the chemical structure does not change.**	Does a chemical or physical change occur? **A solution is a mixture so the chemical structure does not change either.**
Heterogenous and/or Homogenous? Why?: **Mixtures can be heterogenous, mixed so that you can see the different items or homogenous where everything is distributed evenly and it looks like one substance.**	Heterogenous and/or Homogenous? Why?: **Solutions are homogenous. In a solution, everything is mixed and distributed evenly. It looks like one substance.**
Fact/Difference: **Each substance can be separated from a group in physical ways such a filtering.**	Fact/Difference: **A simple solution is basically two substances evenly mixed. One is called the solute (what gets dissolved such as sugar) the other is the solvent (does the dissolving such as water.)**
Fact/Difference: **An alloy is a mixture of metals. An emulsion is a mixture of oils and water.**	Fact/Difference: **Temperature, pressure and structure of substances are all things that can change how things dissolve.**
Examples **Cake, wood in pencil, sand and water, Amalgams, salad dressings**	Examples: **Air, Carbon Dioxide and Soda, Gasoline, Dental Fillings**
Picture: **A picture example of a mixture (answers will vary).**	Picture: **A picture example of a mixture (answers will vary).**

Atom, Molecule or Mixture?
1. Molecules
2. Mixture of Atoms
3. Mixture of Molecules
4. Atoms
5. Mixture of Atoms and Molecules
6. Mixture of Molecules
7. Mixture of Atoms
8. Mixture of Molecules
9. Mixture of Atoms
10. 1, 2, 3, 4
11. 4, 9

Mixtures and Solutions Quiz
1. A
2. A
3. C
4. D
5. C
6. D
7. A
8. C
9. D
10. D
11. B
12. B
13. E
14. A
15. D

Atoms &
Atomic Structure

Atoms & Atomic Structure

This week students will learn about the structure and parts of an atom. They will also learn how scientific theories change and develop.

Keywords:

Atom	Nucleus	Atomic Number	Excited State
Proton	Negative	Reactivity	Atomic Models
Electron	Positive	Energy Levels	
Neutron	Atomic Mass	Ground State	

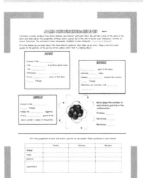

Day 1—Atomic Structure and Interactive Notes

Students will go through an online tutorial to learn about atoms and their structure. Teachers and co-op leaders can project this tutorial and present it similarly to a PowerPoint. You will need to have adobe shockwave installed for this tutorial to play.

Day 2—Rainbow Flame Lab

This is a fun and easy lab. Just make sure you practice fire safety. We like to use a disposable casserole or pie tin for this lab but any heat proof container, like a cookie sheet or glass casserole dish would work. Students will put a spoonful of each chemical (salt, salt substitute, calcium chloride and copper sulfate) on their heat proof plate. These are all safe to burn. Students will then put one squirt of hand sanitizer on the spoonful. The hand sanitizer has alcohol in it that will burn. The salts do not actually burn away from this, so they can be used over and over again as long as more hand sanitizer is added. The electrons of different elements release different colors of light when they have been excited by energy, such as heat, and then fall back to their ground state. The ground state is a lower energy level of the atom. Make sure you discuss fire safety with students and the importance of being cautious and responsible with their movements in the lab. You should have them work in a dim area or a place where you can turn the lights off so that the flame colors can be seen.

!Big !idea *An atom is made of parts that affect its identity and reactivity. Atoms are the building blocks of matter and our theory and model of the atom changes as we learn more.*

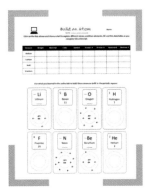

Day 3—Build an Atom Day

This online lab walks students through different elements and teaches students to build their atoms. After completing this lab they should be able to draw the parts of the atoms that are missing at the bottom of the page. In the diagrams, **e–** stands for electron (electrons have negative charges), **p+** stands for proton (protons have positive charges) and **n** stands for neutron (no charge).

Materials:
- **Goggles**
- **Disposable Pie or Casserole Tin (Can reuse for Elephant Toothpaste Lab)**
- **Long Match or Lighter**
- **Pot holder or Small Towel**
- **Calcium Chloride (Damprid)**
- **Copper Sulfate (Root Killer - Home Depot, Ace Hardware, etc)**
- **Hand Sanitizer**
- **Salt Substitute (Potassium Chloride -Grocery Stores)**

Day 4—Atomic History Timeline

Learning about the development of the atomic model not only teachers students about atoms, but it also teaches them how theories and models change as new technologies and observations are made. This is such a great example of good science at work. A scientist knows it is okay to question, to learn more and then revise what you thought was the solution. We recommend a very simple timeline software because it is free and very easy to use. There are other online timeline makers with more features out there that could certainly be used. A paper timeline is always a good thing to make too. If your students want to try something else for their timeline and you have the time for them to do so, this is a good lesson for that. On our resource page tinyurl.com/ybuwjcnx (password: Matter), we have provided some great links for students to use as they research. Students can also search for the information on their own. Caution them away from sites that do not look professional, or any type of wiki or answer site. These are not reliable or accepted sources for a class project. A rubric, for grading, is included on the answer key page.

Day 5—QUIZ: Atoms and Atomic Structure

This is a culmination of the week's learning activities. You can have students study their class work. The test will cover the history of the atomic model, atomic structure and charges and the importance of the atom and its parts. Students should pay special attention to the terms in bold. The vocabulary list in your guide can also help them to prepare. The student notebook does not have a copy of the quiz so you will want to make sure you have the quiz ready for them to take.

Next Generation Science Standards—Unit 5

MS-PS1-1: Develop models to describe the atomic composition of simple molecules and extended structures.
MS-PS1-1: Substances are made from different types of atoms, which combine with one another in various ways. Atoms form molecules that range in size from two to thousands of atoms.
MS-PS1-1-Scale, Proportion, and Quantity: Time, space, and energy phenomena can be observed at various scales using models to study systems that are too large or too small.
MS-PS1-3: Engineering advances have led to important discoveries in virtually every field of science, and scientific discoveries have led to the development of entire industries and engineered systems.

Atomic Structure Interactive Notes Name:

Chemistry is really all about how atoms behave and interact with each other. We will take a look at the parts of the atom and learn about the properties of these atomic pieces. Go to this site to launch your interactive tutorial on Atomic Structure. You will need to have shockwave installed on your computer. tinyurl.com/hfqd8w8

Fill in the blanks as you learn about the three distinct particles that make up an atom. Draw a line from each square to the particle on the picture of the carbon atom that it is talking about.

Proton

- Found in the _____.
- The _____ of protons determines the _____.
- #Protons = _____ _____
- It is a _____ piece of the atom.
- _____ Charge.

Electron

- _____ part of the atom.
- Virtually _____ mass
- Always _____ around the nucleus.
- _____ Charge.
- Electrons are involved in all _____ _____

Neutron

- Found in the _____.
- _____ Charge.
- Holds the _____ together.
- It is a _____ piece of the atom, similar in mass to the proton.

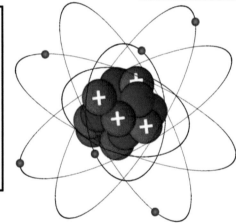

Write down the number of each atomic particle in this carbon atom.

Protons: _____

Electrons: _____

Neutrons: _____

Fill in the properties of each sub atomic particle as you answer these questions in your tutorial.

	Proton	Electron	Neutron
charge			
mass			
location			
importance			

Rainbow Flame Lab

Name:

We are going to heat different compounds and elements with fire to see what color light they produce.

 Lab Safety | **Goggles on! Tie hair back and do not wear loose clothes, long sleeves or jewelry.** This lab involves fire and should be performed with a supervising adult. Use caution and have appropriate safety equipment nearby.

Background Research:

- An atom's electrons stay in **energy levels**. Electrons stay in the lowest energy level they can. Here they are stable and happy, this is called the **ground state**.
- When energy such as fire (heat) is added, the electrons get excited (**excited state**) and jump up levels.
- After being excited they then fall back down to their normal energy levels, releasing energy as **light**.
- Atoms of the metal elements release energy uniquely and different colors of visible light are produced. **The color of this light can be used to identify these elements,** especially when using a spectroscope or prism.
- The ability of metal atoms to produce these colors is used in the making of **fireworks**. By including different metal salts, or mixtures of metal salts, firework manufactures can produce beautiful displays in nearly all the colors of the rainbow.
- These different **colors produced by elements** are also how we **identify what makes a star**. Since we obviously can't visit or send equipment to such an incredibly hot place, we look at the colors of the light spectra coming from stars to identify what makes them.

Materials:

Sodium Chloride (Table Salt)	Potassium Chloride (Salt Substitute)	Copper Sulfate (Root Killer)	Calcium Chloride (Damprid)	Hand Sanitizer (with alcohol)
Goggles	Pot Holder	Spoon	Long Match or Lighter	Disposable pie tin, cookie sheet, etc

Procedure:

1. Put your flame plate (Disposable pie tin, cookie sheet, or something the heat from a fire will not damage) on top of a pot holder to protect your work surface.
2. Place a spoonful of one of the chemical salts on your flame plate.
3. Place one squirt of hand sanitizer on this chemical salt.
4. Dim the lights.
5. Using a long match or a lighter carefully light the hand sanitizer on this chemical salt.
6. Observe the color it burns and record it in the data table below.
   Safety note: Do not use or add more hand sanitizer while the flame is still burning!
7. When the flame completely burns out leave the salt on your flame plate.
8. Repeat steps 1-7 with another chemical salt, placing it in a separate pile from the last chemical salt you tested. Do this until you have flame tested each of your chemical salts.
9. To see all the flaming colors together, add one squirt of hand sanitizer to each of your chemical salts (you do not need to add more) and follow steps 2-5.
10. You can repeat this test as many times as you want. Always make sure the flame is completely burned out before adding more hand sanitizer.

Data Table:

Chemical Salt	Color
Sodium Chloride (Table Salt)	
Potassium Chloride (Salt Substitute)	
Copper Sulfate (Root Killer)	
Calcium Chloride (Damp Rid)	

Questions:

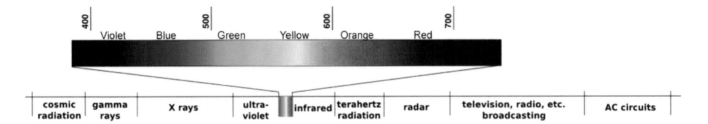

1. Looking at the visible light spectrum, the wavelengths on the right side have a higher frequency and more energy while those on the left side have a lower frequency and lower energy. Which chemical salt's electrons are releasing the most energy as they fall back down to their normal level?

2. A forensic scientist does a flame test on a chemical found at a crime scene. What might they conclude if the light emitted by the substance is green?

3. What is the normal, most stable state for an atom's electrons to be in?

4. What is an electron's state when energy is added and the electron jumps up a level?

5. Explain how the colors in a flame test are produced.

6. Why is a flame test an important lab tool?

Build an Atom

Go to: tinyurl.com/y9gds3lh

Name: _____

Click on the link above and choose start to explore different atoms and their elements. Fill out this data table as you complete the online lab.

Element	Weight	Material	Color	Symbol	Atomic #	Proton #	Neutron #	Electron #
Helium								
Carbon								
Gold								
Uranium								

Use what you learned in the online lab to build these atoms or to fill in the periodic square:

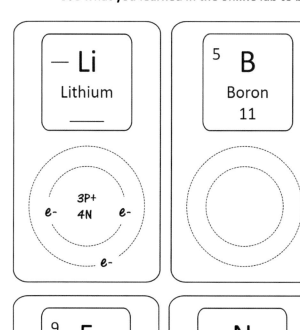

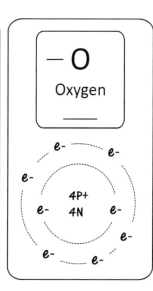

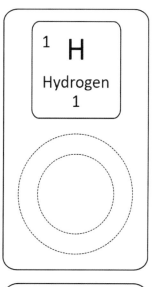

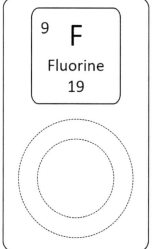

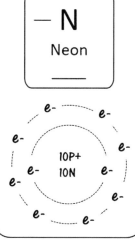

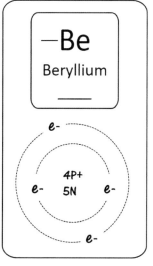

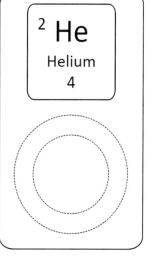

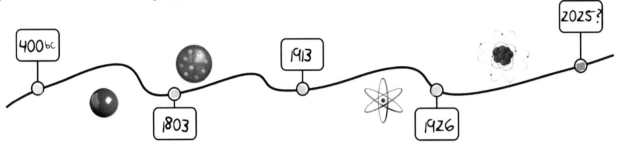

Atomic History Timeline

You are going to create an online timeline to show how the atomic theory has changed over time and to highlight scientists who contributed to the atomic theory. You will use a timeline maker by ReadWriteThink; it is simple and free. You can also opt to create this timeline using any other online timeline tool, or even draw it out on paper.

As you learn about the history of the Atomic Theory you see the scientific process in action. As scientists solidify their theories they share them with the scientific community. Other scientists test and build upon these theories using new technologies and ideas. This can lead to a new theory. In science, we are always trying to further our knowledge by experimenting, learning and sharing.

Watch this short video on the history of the atom: tinyurl.com/mpnk5k3

Listed below are the six models of the atom and seven scientists who greatly contributed to our understanding of the atomic theory.

- Democritus
- John Dalton
- J.J. Thomson

- Ernest Rutherford
- Niels Bohr
- De Broglie / Schrodinger

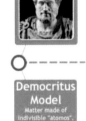

For each of the seven scientists above you must include:
- As the label: their name and either the date of the scientist's birth or of theory.
- As the short description: one sentence description of them, in your own words.
- A picture.
- Place links to any of your sources in the full description box.

For each of the six atomic models you must include:
- Name of model as your label.
- A one sentence description of this model in your own words, for the short description.
- A picture example.
- Credit your sources by placing links to them in your sources in the "full description" box.

Research Tips: When searching online you might get better results if you include the words "atomic theory" in your searches. For example "atomic theory history" or "Democritus atomic theory." You can find this information by searching online. Some sites we recommend for good information are on our resource page tinyurl.com/ybuwjcnx (password: Matter). When you search make sure that you are using reputable sites. Ask sites and wiki sites are generally poor or unacceptable sources of information for a class project.

To make your timeline go to: tinyurl.com/qf2xxn2
Click on the button to allow adobe flash. If you do not have this program you will need to download adobe flash.
- Click on the timeline to add a scientist or atomic model. If you need help, click on the "?" for a quick tour and explanation of how to add your information.
- Arrange your timeline so that the scientists and models are in the correct order.
- When you are finished click save and follow the instructions to save the file to your computer.

  Picture tip: When you find a picture online, right click on it and choose "save as" to save the picture to your computer. You will then be able to upload your pictures to your online timeline.

Atoms and Atomic Structure Quiz

Name:

Thomson's Atomic Model

Rutherford's Atomic Model

Current Atomic Model

Multiple Choice
Identify the choice that best completes the statement or answers the question.

_____ 1. Which of these statements about the above figure is most likely correct?
    a. The atomic model has changed very little over time.
    c. Scientists are still debating which of the three theories is correct.
    b. The current model is completely different from the past models of the atom.
    d. As scientists learned more, they modified the theory of the atomic model.

_____ 2. Which statement about the atomic nucleus is correct?
    a. The nucleus is made of protons and neutrons and has a negative charge.
    c. The nucleus is made of electrons and has a negative charge.
    b. The nucleus is made of protons and neutrons and has a positive charge.
    d. The nucleus is made of electrons and has a positive charge.

_____ 3. Balanced atoms do not have an electric charge because they _____.
    a. have an equal number of electrons and protons.
    c. have an equal number of neutrons and protons.
    b. have an equal number of charged and noncharged particles.
    d. have neutrons in the nucleus.

_____ 4. The basic building blocks of matter are _____.
    a. neutrons.
    c. atoms.
    b. protons.
    d. electrons.

_____ 5. The first person who suggested that matter was made up of atoms that were indivisible was the Greek philosopher _____.
    a. Thomson
    c. Democritus
    b. Aristotle
    d. Plato

Matching
Match one or more of the choices that best complete the statement or answer the question.

a. Protons   b. Electrons   c. Neutrons   d. Valance Electrons   e. Element
f. Negative   g. Positive   h. Nucleus   i. Atomic Number   j. Atomic Mass

_____ 6. The number of this determines what an element is.

_____ 7. Balanced atom's have equal numbers of protons and _____.

_____ 8. John Dalton's atomic theory state's that atoms of the same _____ are exactly alike.

_____ 9. The nucleus of an atom has a _____ charge.

_____ 10. Neutron's and protons are found in the _____ of an atom.

_____ 11. Responsible for an atom's reactivity.

_____ 12. Are heavy and hold the nucleus together.

Match the choices above to the part of the atom it best represents.

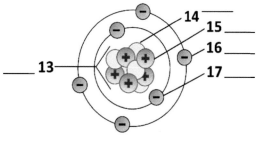

_____ 13

14 _____
15 _____
16 _____
17 _____

Answer Key—Unit 5: Atoms & Atomic Structure

Atomic Structure Interactive Notes

Protons
1. Nucleus
2. Number; Element
3. Atomic Number
4. Heavy
5. +1

Neutron
1. Nucleus
2. 0
3. Protons or Nucleus
4. Heavy

Electron
1. Smallest
2. No or 0
3. Moving
4. -1
5. Chemical Reactions

Particles in Carbon Atom:
1. Protons= 6
2. Electrons=6
3. Neutrons=6

Fill in Table:
Proton: +1, Heavy, Nucleus, determines identity of the atom
Electron: -1, virtually 0, outside nucleus, responsible for reactivity
Neutron: 0, heavy, in nucleus, holds together nucleus

Rainbow Flame Lab

Sodium Chloride = Yellow Flame
Potassium Chloride= Purple Flame
Copper Sulfate= Green Flame
Calcium Chloride=Orange Flame

1. Calcium Chloride glows orange. This is the highest frequency out of all the colors produced so this chemical's electrons release the most energy as they fall back down to their normal level.
2. That it is copper sulfate
3. In the ground state, at the lowest energy level.
4. The electron is in the excited state.
5. An element's electrons get excited by the heat energy added. Because of this they jump up energy levels. When the electron's fall back down to their ground state they release energy in the form of light. Each element's electrons release a different frequency or color of light.
6. Since each element releases its own color of light this can help us identify mystery substances or even what makes up things we cannot touch or reach, such as a star.

Build an Atom

Helium: Helium; Light; Gas; Colorless; He; 2; 2; 2
Carbon: Carbon; Light; Solid; Black; C; 6; 6; 6
Gold: Gold; Heavy; Solid; Yellow; Au; 79; 79; 118
Uranium: Uranium; Heavy; Solid; Silvery white; U; 92; 92; 146

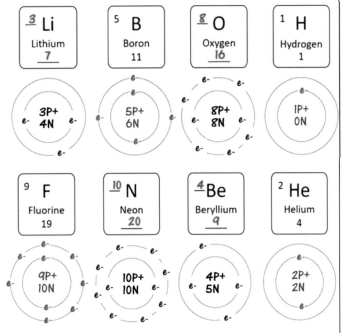

Atomic History Timeline Rubric

Scientists	Name	Date	Description	Picture	Points
Democritus	1	1	1	1	
Dalton	1	1	1	1	
Thomson	1	1	1	1	
Rutherford	1	1	1	1	
Bohr	1	1	1	1	
Debroglie	1	1	1	1	
Schrodinger	1	1	1	1	
Models	**Name**	**Description**		**Picture**	
Democritus	1	1.5		1	
Dalton	1	1.5		1	
Thomson	1	1.5		1	
Rutherford	1	1.5		1	
Bohr	1	1.5		1	
Debroglie/ Schrodinger	1	1.5		1	
Title		1			
Total Points					**/50**

Atomic History Timeline Example on Next Page

Atoms and Atomic Structure Quiz

1. D
2. B
3. A
4. C
5. C
6. A
7. B
8. E
9. G
10. H
11. B or D
12. C
13. H
14. C
15. A
16. D
17. B

Example Timeline

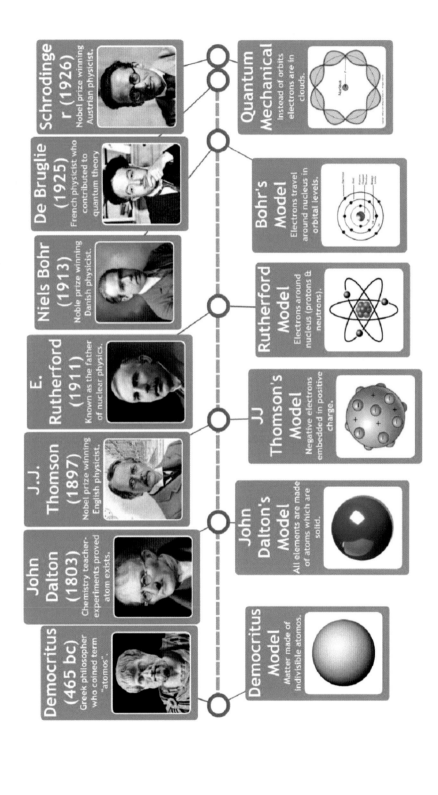

The Periodic Table

The Periodic Table

This week students will learn about the periodic table and its arrangement. They will learn that the arrangement of the periodic has a lot to tell us about each element.

Keywords:

Periodic Table	Atomic Mass	Rare Earth Metals	Halogens
Periods	Atomic Weight	Actinide Metals	Noble Gases
Groups	Alkali Metals	Poor Metals	Valance Electrons
Families	Alkali Earth Metals	Metalloids	Energy Levels
Atomic Symbol	Transition Metals	Nonmetals	

Day 1—A Special Table

The way the periodic table is arranged creates a really cool code that tells us about each element. Students will be introduced to the arrangement of the periodic table and its families, groups and periods as they watch a 14 minute video. If you watch this with your co-op or class we recommend pausing at 6:44 so that students have enough time to label their periodic table. Students will then watch a fun video on the 10 strangest elements. They should pick 3 to write notes on in the table provided for them.

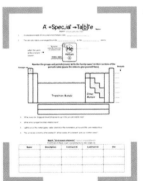

Day 2—Periodic Scavenger Hunt

We have found a colorful, interactive table for students to explore. They will familiarize themselves with the periodic table and elements as they hunt around this interactive periodic table. Students will be looking for trends and learning about specific elements and families. We recommend having students complete this individually but if that is not an option you could project the interactive table on a screen and complete it as a group.

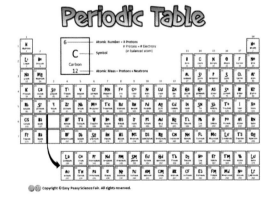

Copyright © Easy Peasy Science Fair. All rights reserved.

You can make predictions about the behavior of atoms of an element based on its position in the periodic table.

Day 3—Atom's Family Electrons

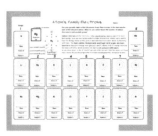

Valance electrons play a huge role in whether or not an atom will chemically react with other atoms. Students will draw model atoms showing their placement in the periodic table. This will allow them to see a trend in the number of valance electrons in each periodic group and why certain groups are more reactive than others.

Materials:
- **2 Dry Erase Markers**
- **2 File or Regular Folders**
- **4 Laminated Periodic Tables** (Can use page protectors instead of laminating.)
- **Tape**

Day 4—Periodic Table Battleship

This is a fun review game and will further familiarize students with the placement of elements in the periodic table. Print out and laminate 4 copies of our periodic table and use folders to set up the game. Laminate or cover the periodic tables with page protectors so that students can write on them with their dry erase markers. Students will call out atomic symbols to play. They can also change it up and play another game calling out atomic numbers, atomic masses, or number of protons or neutrons. This game requires two players. Students can play with a sibling, classmate or even a parent. Have the student "teach" the other player the information they need to know about the periodic table to play.

Day 5—QUIZ: Periodic Table

Students will need to use a periodic table for this quiz. This is a culmination of the week's learning activities. You can have students study their class work. The test will cover the arrangement of the periodic table as well as its groups, rows and families. They will need to be able identify the characteristics of elements from their location on the periodic table. Students should also recognize and be able to build a model of an atom just from its periodic square. Students should pay special attention to the terms in bold. The vocabulary list in your guide can also help them to prepare. The student notebook does not have a copy of the quiz so you will want to make sure you have the quiz ready for them to take.

Next Generation Science Standards—Unit 6

HS-PS1-1: Use the periodic table as a model to predict the relative properties of elements based on the patterns of electrons in the outermost energy level of atoms.
MS-PS1-1: Time, space, and energy phenomena can be observed at various scales using models to study systems that are too large or too small.
MS-PS1-1; MS-PS1-4: Develop a model to predict and/or describe phenomena.
MS-PS1-3; MS-PS1-2: Each pure substance has characteristic physical and chemical properties.
MPS1-3: given conditions) that can be used to identify it. Structures can be designed to serve particular functions by taking into account properties of different materials, and how materials can be shaped and used.

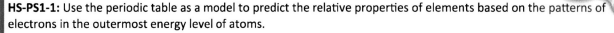

Periodic Table

Groups

Periods

Legend:
- **Atomic Number = # Protons**
- **# Protons = # Electrons** (in balanced atom)
- **Symbol**
- **Atomic Mass = Protons + Neutrons**

Example:
6
C
Carbon
12

Group 1	2	3	4	5	6	7	8	9	10	11	12	13	14	15	16	17	18
1 **H** Hydrogen 1																	2 **He** Helium 4
3 **Li** Lithium 7	4 **Be** Beryllium 9											5 **B** Boron 11	6 **C** Carbon 12	7 **N** Nitrogen 14	8 **O** Oxygen 16	9 **F** Fluorine 19	10 **Ne** Neon 20
11 **Na** Sodium 23	12 **Mg** Magnesium 24											13 **Al** Aluminum 27	14 **Si** Silicon 28	15 **P** Phosphorus 31	16 **S** Sulfur 32	17 **Cl** Chlorine 35	18 **Ar** Argon 40
19 **K** Potassium 39	20 **Ca** Calcium 40	21 **Sc** Scandium 45	22 **Ti** Titanium 48	23 **V** Vanadium 51	24 **Cr** Chromium 52	25 **Mn** Manganese 55	26 **Fe** Iron 56	27 **Co** Cobalt 59	28 **Ni** Nickel 59	29 **Cu** Copper 64	30 **Zn** Zinc 65	31 **Ga** Gallium 70	32 **Ge** Germanium 73	33 **As** Arsenic 75	34 **Se** Selenium 79	35 **Br** Bromine 80	36 **Kr** Krypton 84
37 **Rb** Rubidium 85	38 **Sr** Strontium 88	39 **Y** Yttrium 89	40 **Zr** Zirconium 91	41 **Nb** Niobium 93	42 **Mo** Molybdenum 96	43 **Tc** Technetium 98	44 **Ru** Ruthenium 101	45 **Rh** Rhodium 103	46 **Pd** Palladium 106	47 **Ag** Silver 108	48 **Cd** Cadmium 112	49 **In** Indium 115	50 **Sn** Tin 119	51 **Sb** Antimony 122	52 **Te** Tellurium 128	53 **I** Iodine 127	54 **Xe** Xenon 131
55 **Cs** Caesium 133	56 **Ba** Barium 137	57 **La** Lanthanum 139	72 **Hf** Hafnium 178	73 **Ta** Tantalum 181	74 **W** Tungsten 184	75 **Re** Rhenium 186	76 **Os** Osmium 190	77 **Ir** Iridium 192	78 **Pt** Platinum 195	79 **Au** Gold 197	80 **Hg** Mercury 201	81 **Tl** Thallium 204	82 **Pb** Lead 207	83 **Bi** Bismuth 209	84 **Po** Polonium 209	85 **At** Astatine 210	86 **Rn** Radon 222
87 **Fr** Francium 223	88 **Ra** Radium 226	89 **Ac** Actinium 227	104 **Rf** Rutherfordium 267	105 **Db** Dubnium 268	106 **Sg** Seaborgium 269	107 **Bh** Bohrium 270	108 **Hs** Hassium 277	109 **Mt** Meitnerium 278	110 **Ds** Darmstadtium 281	111 **Rg** Roentgenium 282	112 **Cn** Copernicium 285	113 **Nh** Nihonium 286	114 **Fl** Flerovium 289	115 **Mc** Moscovium 290	116 **Lv** Livermorium 293	117 **Ts** Tennessine 294	118 **Og** Oganesson 294

Lanthanides:

57 **La** Lanthanum 139	58 **Ce** Cerium 140	59 **Pr** Praseodymium 141	60 **Nd** Neodymium 144	61 **Pm** Promethium 145	62 **Sm** Samarium 150	63 **Eu** Europium 152	64 **Gd** Gadolinium 157	65 **Tb** Terbium 159	66 **Dy** Dysprosium 163	67 **Ho** Holmium 165	68 **Er** Erbium 167	69 **Tm** Thulium 169	70 **Yb** Ytterbium 173	71 **Lu** Lutetium 175

Actinides:

89 **Ac** Actinium 227	90 **Th** Thorium 232	91 **Pa** Protactinium 231	92 **U** Uranium 238	93 **Np** Neptunium 237	94 **Pu** Plutonium 244	95 **Am** Americium 243	96 **Cm** Curium 247	97 **Bk** Berkelium 247	98 **Cf** Californium 251	99 **Es** Einsteinium 252	100 **Fm** Fermium 257	101 **Md** Mendelevium 258	102 **No** Nobelium 259	103 **Lr** Lawrencium 266

Printable available on Online Resource page

Å +Spec₊iål →Ta⬚b⬚l̊e

Watch: tinyurl.com/qfvnhkm

1. A substance made of only one kind of atom is an: _____

2. The periodic table is arranged from the _____ to the _____ atoms.

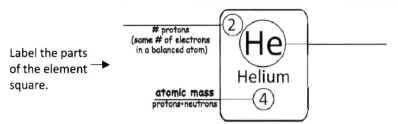

Label the parts of the element square. →

protons
(same # of electrons in a balanced atom)

② He
Helium

atomic mass
protons+neutrons
④

Number the groups and periods (rows). Write the family name's in their sections of the periodic table (pause the video to give yourself time).

Groups→ ____

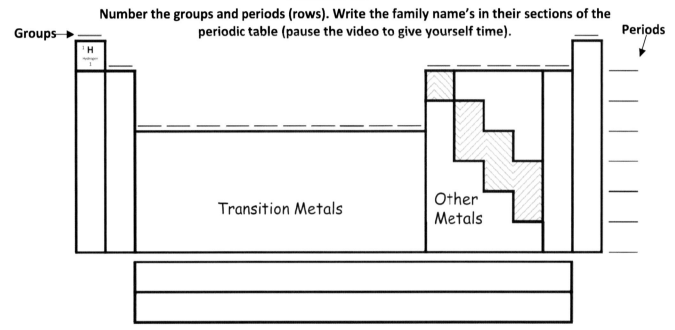

Transition Metals

Other Metals

Periods ____

3. What does the diagonal band of elements split the periodic table into?

4. What are 4 properties that metals have?

5. Lightly color the metals gray. Label and color the nonmetals yellow and the semimetals blue.

6. The universe is mostly what element? What makes this element special in other ways?

Watch "10 strangest elements": tinyurl.com/ybt9qwh3
Pick three of these super cool elements to take notes on.

Name	Description	Cool Fact #1	Cool Fact #2	Use

Periodic Scavenger Hunt

Name:

Click on the element squares of this site to label this periodic table and to answer the questions below. You will notice that some families such as the semi-metals in your notes are called metalloids.

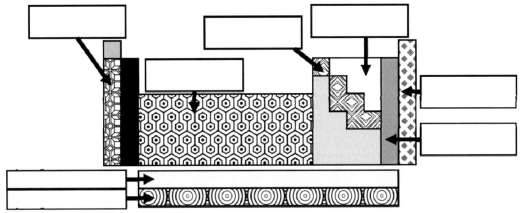

1. Click on Lithium. What are three examples of how we use lithium?

    •   What color is lithium in its purest form? Is it a Solid, Liquid or Gas? (**hint:** click interactive for the symbol key.)

    •   Lithium is in the Alkali Metal family. What are 3 facts about Alkali Metals? Include what Lithium catches fire with.

2. Which elements are Alkali metals? List their symbols: _____ _____ _____ _____ _____ _____

3. What are 3 characteristics of Alkali Earth Metals? How reactive are they?

4. Describe Calcium. What color is it in its purest form?

5. If you wanted to conduct electricity well would you use a Transition Metal or an Alkali Earth Metal?

6. List three examples of a transition metal. From their description do you think they are reactive?

7. Do poor metals melt more easily than transition metals? Between Gallium and Zinc which do you think will have a lower melting point?

8. What is special about Metalloids? Do they conduct electricity?

9. Which elements are Metalloids? List their symbols: _____ _____ _____ _____ _____ _____

10. What does the term "Halogen" mean?

11. What is something Noble Gases never do? Why is this?

12. Which is your favorite Noble Gas? Why?

13. What is unique about Hydrogen's periodic family (group)?

14. How much of the universe is made of Hydrogen atoms?

15. Which elements are gases at room temperature? ___ ___ ___ ___ ___ ___ ___ ___ ___ ___ ___

Check out some of these awesome periodic table videos by the university of Nottingham. Here you can see real elements and how they react and even explode! periodicvideos.com

74

Atom's Family Electrons

Name: _____

Use your periodic table to find the atomic # and then to draw in the electrons for each of the elements below. **What do you notice about the number of valance electrons in each periodic group?**

Valance electrons are the electrons in the <u>outside energy level or shell</u> of an atom. Each energy level can only hold a certain number of electrons. Atoms really want to have full energy levels, so they give or take electrons from other atoms by bonding with them. The **most reactive elements only need to get rid of or gain one more electron** to have a full energy level (groups 1 and 7). Atoms with full energy levels do not bond with other atoms and are not reactive (**ex: group 8: noble gases**).
As you move down to the 4th and 5th periods of the periodic table the atoms will have more levels. We are focusing on the first 3 periods because they are easier to draw.

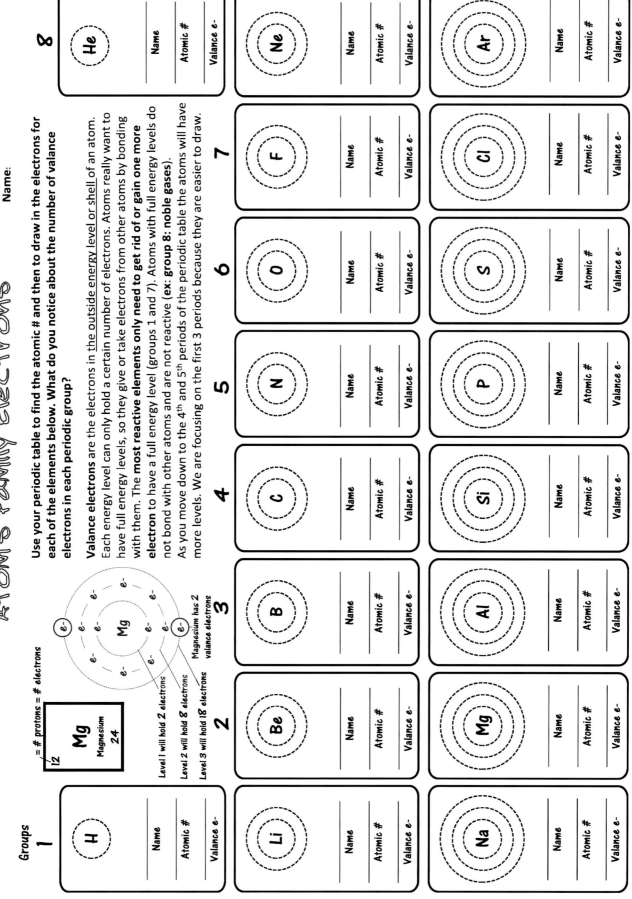

= # protons = # electrons

Mg
Magnesium
24

12

Level 1 will hold **2** electrons
Level 2 will hold **8** electrons
Level 3 will hold **18** electrons

Magnesium has **2** valance electrons

Groups

1

He

Name _____
Atomic # _____
Valance e- _____

2

Be

Name _____
Atomic # _____
Valance e- _____

3

B

Name _____
Atomic # _____
Valance e- _____

4

C

Name _____
Atomic # _____
Valance e- _____

5

N

Name _____
Atomic # _____
Valance e- _____

6

O

Name _____
Atomic # _____
Valance e- _____

7

F

Name _____
Atomic # _____
Valance e- _____

8

He

Name _____
Atomic # _____
Valance e- _____

H

Name _____
Atomic # _____
Valance e- _____

Li

Name _____
Atomic # _____
Valance e- _____

Na

Name _____
Atomic # _____
Valance e- _____

Mg

Name _____
Atomic # _____
Valance e- _____

Al

Name _____
Atomic # _____
Valance e- _____

Si

Name _____
Atomic # _____
Valance e- _____

P

Name _____
Atomic # _____
Valance e- _____

S

Name _____
Atomic # _____
Valance e- _____

Cl

Name _____
Atomic # _____
Valance e- _____

Ne

Name _____
Atomic # _____
Valance e- _____

Ar

Name _____
Atomic # _____
Valance e- _____

75

Periodic Table Battleship

You are going to play battleship using your periodic table! Try to hit your opponent's battle ships by calling out the elements or the groups and periods. The first one to sink all the ships wins!

Play this game like traditional battleship in groups of two. Each player will have their folder open so that their opponent cannot see their periodic tables.

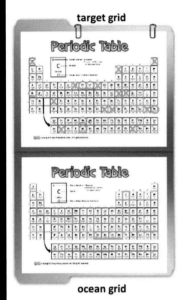

target grid

ocean grid

1. Use your marker to outline your element ships on the "ocean grid". You can place your ship either vertical or horizontal, not diagonal.
   - 1 Aircraft Carrier = 5 elements
   - 2 Battleships = 4 elements
   - 2 Submarines = 3 elements
   - 1 PT boat = 2 elements
2. The first player takes a shot calling the period and group for the element of their choice. The other player states the name of the element called, to confirm, and then says "hit" or "miss."
3. Mark hits on the "target" grid by circling the elements and place an **X** on the elements for misses. These are your guesses.
4. As your opponent calls their shots, mark their hits and misses on your ocean grid to help you keep track of what they are doing.
5. If all the elements of a ship have been guessed, it is sunk. Let your opponent know when they sink a ship.
6. The first player to sink all opposing ships wins the game!

Try playing again. This time calling out the atomic symbols, atomic numbers or masses. You can also play by calling out the number of protons or neutrons, for a challenge.

Student instructions

Practice your periodic table skills as you play this fun game. Once this game is over you should be able to locate elements on the periodic table by their atomic symbol and their position on the table.

Play time: 20-30 minutes
Materials for 2 Players:
- 2 file folders
- 2 dry erase markers
- 4 large paper clips or tape
- 4 copies of the periodic table, laminated
  (You can also use page protectors or in a pinch you can use a gallon Ziploc bag or cover them with saranwrap.)

Vocabulary:

Atomic Symbol	Protons
Atomic Mass	Electrons
Period	Neutron
Groups	

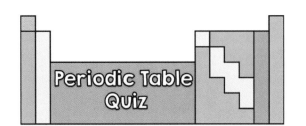

Multiple Choice

Identify the choice that best completes the statement or answers the question. **You should use your periodic table.**

____ 1. Atoms of elements that are in the same group have the same number of _____.

    a. neutrons.   b. protons and neutrons.   c. protons.   d. valence electrons.

____ 2. Valence electrons determine an atom's _____.

    a. chemical reactivity.   b. period.   c. electric charge.   d. mass.

____ 3. An atom's mass number equals the number of _____.

    a. neutrons.   b. protons.   c. protons plus neutrons.   d. protons plus electrons.

____ 4. Which of the following elements is an alkali earth metal?

    a. mercury   b. sodium   c. calcium   d. magnesium

____ 5. The properties of a substance, such as water, are determined by the type, number, and _____.

    a. speed of its atoms.   b. nature of its atoms.   c. speed of its protons.   d. arrangement of its atoms.

____ 6. What are the number of neutrons in an atom of Osmium?

    a. 190   b. 114   c. 8   d. 76

____ 7. How many electrons are in a balanced atom of Gallium?

    a. 13   b. 70   c. 39   d. 31

____ 8. The order of elements in the periodic table is based upon the number of _____ an atom has.

    a. electrons   b. nucleus   c. neutrons   d. protons

____ 9. Which of these atoms is the element Boron?

    a.   b.   c.   d.

____ 10. Which statement about noble gases is correct?

    a. They form compounds with very bright colors.   c. They are extremely rare in nature.

    b. They exist as single atoms rather than as molecules because they do not need to react with other atoms.   d. They are highly reactive with both metals and nonmetals because they do not have enough electrons for a full outer shell.

Matching

Use your periodic table and what you know about each family to match one or more of the choices that best complete the statement or answer the question.

    a. Hg   b. Fr   c. Kr   d. Rh   e. H   f. S

____ 11. A nonmetal that gives eggs, onions and skunks their smell.

____ 12. If Susan wanted to find an element that would conduct electricity, which would she pick?

____ 13. This element is liquid at room temperature

____ 14. The lightest and most abundant element in the universe.

____ 15. Alex wants to find a chemical so reactive that it will even react and catch fire with water. What is the most reactive element listed?

____ 16. Which element is a Noble Gas?

Answer Key—Unit 6: The Periodic Table

A Special Table
1. Elements
2. Lightest to the heaviest

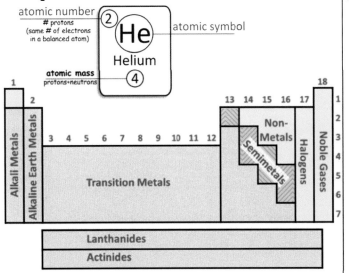

3. Metals and Non-Metals
4. Conduct electricity, shiny, malleable, hard
5. Look at colors in table above.
6. Hydrogen: not a metal, group all by itself, is a gas at room temperature.

10 Strangest Elements: answers will vary but the table should be filled in for three of the elements in the video.

Periodic Scavenger Hunt

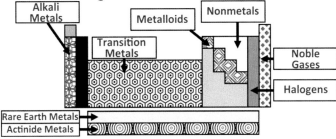

1. Batteries, impact resistant ceramic cookware, mood stabilizer, lightweight aluminum alloys
   * Metallic, solid
   * Very reactive, very soft, not foud free in nature, catches fire with water
2. Li, Na, K, Rb, Cs, Fr
3. Reactive, not found free in nature, soft and somewhat brittle metals
4. Metallic, soft metal found in shells, bones, milk, etc
5. Transition Metal
6. Answers will vary but should be from transition metal section. From the descriptions they do not seem reactive.
7. Melt easily, have a lower melting point than transition metals
8. They are partly like metals and partly like nonmetals; conduct electricity in some conditions
9. B, Si, Ge, As, Te, Sb
10. Salt-former
11. Bond with other atoms. Each atom has exactly the number of electrons it needs in its outer shell.
12. Answers will vary but should be from Noble Gas group
13. It is in its own group.
14. 90%
15. H, He, Ne, Ar, Kr, Xe, Rn, F, Cl, O, N

Atom's Family Electron Key on Next Page

Periodic Table Quiz
1. D
2. A
3. C
4. C
5. D
6. B
7. D
8. D
9. B
10. B
11. F
12. A, D
13. A
14. E
15. B
16. C

Atom's Family Electrons KEY

Use your periodic table to find the atomic # and then to draw in the electrons for each of the elements below. **What do you notice about the number of valence electrons in each periodic group?**

Each group has the same # of valence electrons. These are important to chemical reactions that it affects how the periodic table is organized.

Valence electrons are the electrons in the outside energy level or shell of an atom. Each energy level can only hold a certain number of electrons. Atoms really want to have full energy levels, so they give or take electrons from other atoms by bonding with them. **The most reactive elements only need to get rid of or gain one more electron** to have a full energy level (groups 1 and 7). Atoms with full energy levels do not bond with other atoms and are not reactive (**ex: group 8: noble gases**). As you move down to the 4th and 5th periods of the periodic table the atoms will have more levels. We are focusing on the first 3 periods because they are easier to draw.

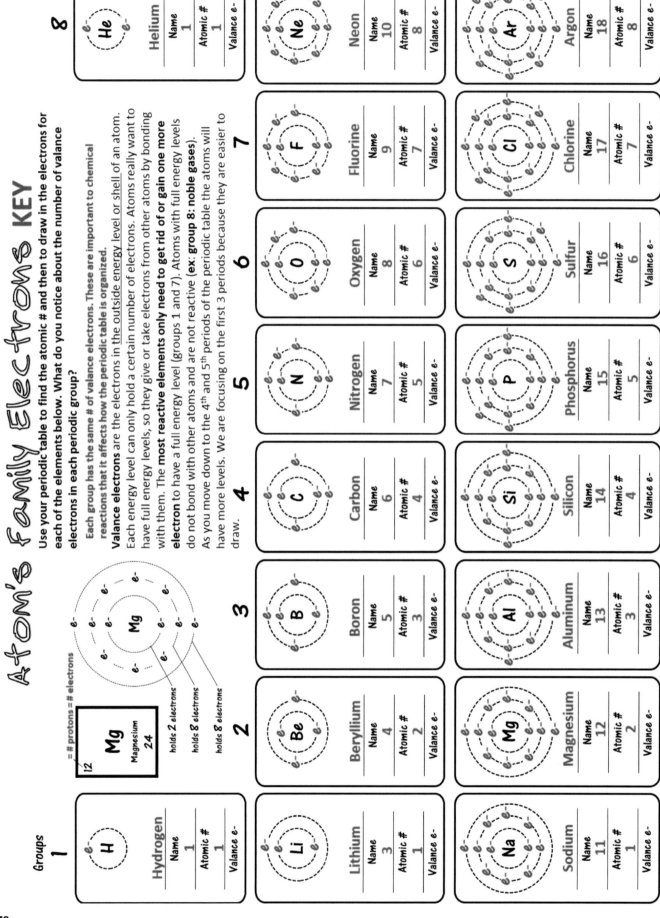

Groups

1

He — Helium — Name 1 — Atomic # 1 — Valance e- — **8**

H — Hydrogen — Name 1 — Atomic # 1 — Valance e-

== # protons = # electrons

12 | **Mg** | Magnesium | 24

holds 2 electrons
holds 8 electrons
holds 8 electrons

Li — Lithium — Name 3 — Atomic # 1 — Valance e-

Be — Beryllium — Name 4 — Atomic # 2 — Valance e- — **2**

B — Boron — Name 5 — Atomic # 3 — Valance e- — **3**

C — Carbon — Name 6 — Atomic # 4 — Valance e- — **4**

N — Nitrogen — Name 7 — Atomic # 5 — Valance e- — **5**

O — Oxygen — Name 8 — Atomic # 6 — Valance e- — **6**

F — Fluorine — Name 9 — Atomic # 7 — Valance e- — **7**

Ne — Neon — Name 10 — Atomic # 8 — Valance e-

Na — Sodium — Name 11 — Atomic # 1 — Valance e-

Mg — Magnesium — Name 12 — Atomic # 2 — Valance e-

Al — Aluminum — Name 13 — Atomic # 3 — Valance e-

Si — Silicon — Name 14 — Atomic # 4 — Valance e-

P — Phosphorus — Name 15 — Atomic # 5 — Valance e-

S — Sulfur — Name 16 — Atomic # 6 — Valance e-

Cl — Chlorine — Name 17 — Atomic # 7 — Valance e-

Ar — Argon — Name 18 — Atomic # 8 — Valance e-

Physical Properties & Changes

Physical Properties & Changes

This week students will learn about different physical properties and that a physical change does not change a substance chemically but is merely a change in color, state, shape, etc.

Keywords:

Physical Properties	State of Matter	Buoyance	Density
Physical Changes	Luster	Conductor	Solubility
Viscosity	Ductility	Magnetic	Malleability
Freezing Point	Volume	Mixture	Mass

Day 1—Physical Properties Cut and Paste Vocabulary + Melting Styrofoam Demo

To introduce physical properties and changes perform the "Melting Styrofoam Demo," and discuss this cool physical change. Students will then complete "Physical Properties Cut and Paste." This cut an paste vocabulary activity is a hands on and visual technique for learning important terms. Students can use the internet to search for these terms and then match the pictures and definitions. They can also use a dictionary, encyclopedia or an old textbook.

Day 2—Ooey Gooey Oobleck Lab

Kids love this lab and the oobleck is a fun thing to play with even after the lab is done. Oobleck is a non-Newtonian fluid, meaning that it has both solid and liquid properties because of this it will be interesting to explore its physical properties. Borax can be purchased in the laundry section of your grocery store and is nontoxic. We always caution our students to carefully follow the directions for this lab and to be careful with the amount of food coloring (Just saying that out loud makes a difference!). You do want to keep the oobleck away from fabric and rugs, because it will stick. You can use vinegar to remove it. Oobleck will keep well for several weeks if stored in the refrigerator.

We broke this lab into parts in case a classroom or co-op teacher wanted to prepare the liquids themselves. You can make up a batch of the glue and water and a batch of the borax and water ahead of time. Students can then just measure and combine these two liquids and the food coloring.

!Big !idea *Physical changes alter physical properties of substances but do not change the chemical composition of the substance.*

Day 3—Density Challenge Online Lab

Students will find the density of different objects online using a scale and a graduated cylinder. These are important scientific tools for students to use and become familiar with. We know that many people will not have these at home and wanted students to at least get to use them virtually. Density is a very important physical property of matter which is found by dividing mass by the volume.

Materials:
- Food Coloring
- Borax (walmart, grocery store, etc)
- White Elmer's Glue
- Measuring spoons
- Styrofoam Cup
- Acetone (Home Improvement Store)

Day 4—Physical Properties of Matter Prezi Project

Creating a presentation is a fantastic way for students to learn technology skills and an interesting way for them to learn. Prezi is a really fun and free presentation resource. Students will need an email address to sign up. They can use a parent email if they do not have their own. On our resource page tinyurl.com/ybuwjcnx (password: Matter), we have provided some great links for students to use as they research. Students can also search for the information on their own. Caution them away from sites that do not look professional, or any type of wiki or answer site. These are not reliable or accepted sources for a class project.

Day 5—Finish Prezi Project and PRESENTATION

Students can take some time to finish their prezi and then present it for their quiz grade. This project covers physical properties and changes and ties them into everyday life. This presentation incorporates technology into the unit. A rubric is included on the answer key page.

Next Generation Science Standards—Unit 7

MS-PS1-2: Analyze and interpret data on the properties of substances before and after the substances interact to determine if a chemical reaction has occurred.

MS-PS1-2; MS-PS1-3: Each pure substance has characteristic physical and chemical properties (for any bulk quantity under given conditions) that can be used to identify it.

MS-PS1-3: Gather, read, and synthesize information from multiple appropriate sources and assess the credibility, accuracy, and possible bias of each publication and methods used, and describe how they are supported or now supported by evidence.

MS-PS1-3: Structures can be designed to serve particular functions by taking into account properties of different materials, and how materials can be shaped and used.

Melting Styrofoam Cup Demo

A Physical Change Demo

Materials:

- Glass dish or pie plate
- Acetone— Available at home improvement stores
- Styrofoam Cup

Caution: This experiment involves a strong chemical. Wear safety glasses and perform this experiment in a well ventilated area, such as a large room or outdoors.

Introduction:

1. Dramatically rip a paper in half and ask students if ripping the paper changes it into a new substance. They should tell you that it is still paper even though it is ripped.

2. Explain that a physical change is any change that does not actually change what a substance is. Have them give examples of some other physical changes that could be made such as: cutting, bending, melting, freezing, crushing and mixing.

3. Ask students if popping a balloon would be a physical change? Yes it is because you just released air from the rubber balloon. The rubber has not changed, neither has the air.

4. Show students your Styrofoam cup and tell students that you are going to take the air out of it. Styrofoam is actually a polymer called polystyrene. The polystyrene polymer is a long chain of molecules that can hold pockets of air just like a balloon.

What to Do:

1. Pour a thin layer of acetone so that it covers the bottom of your glass dish or pie plate.
2. Put your Styrofoam cup in it and watch it melt!

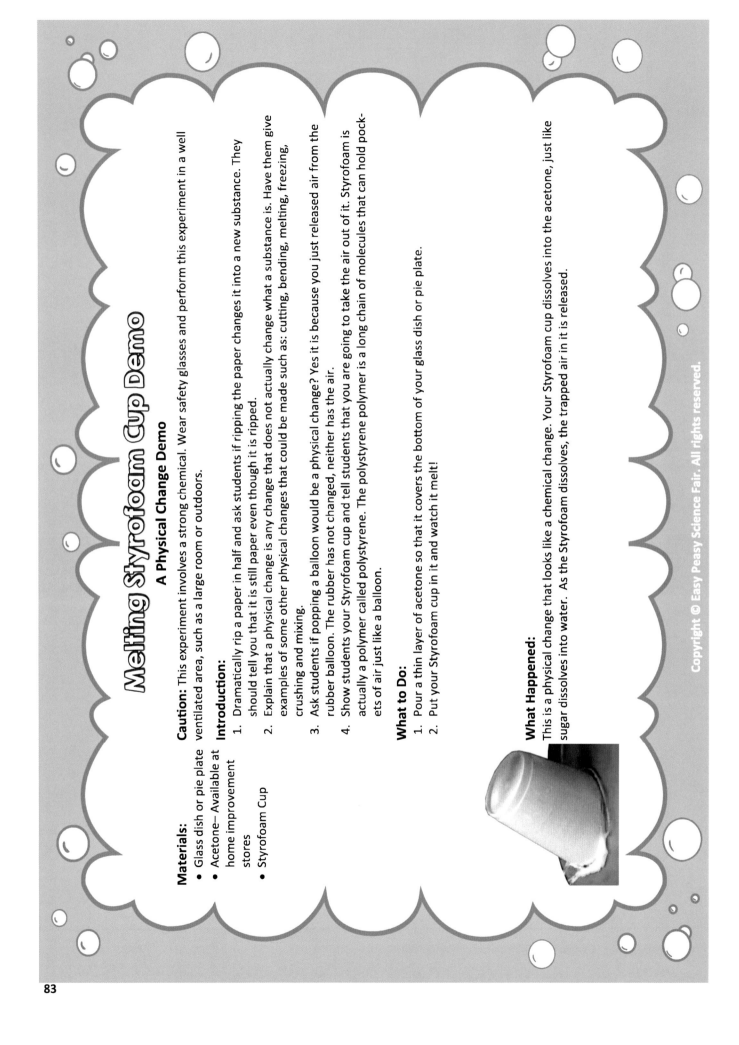

What Happened:

This is a physical change that looks like a chemical change. Your Styrofoam cup dissolves into the acetone, just like sugar dissolves into water. As the Styrofoam dissolves, the trapped air in it is released.

Physical Property Vocab

Cut and paste the definitions and pictures that go with these physical properties.   Name:

You can use the internet or resource books to find the definitions.

#			
1	Physical Properties		
2	Viscosity		
3	Freezing Point		
4	State of Matter		
5	Luster		
6	Ductility		
7	Volume		
8	Buoyancy		
9	Conductor		
10	Magnetic		
11	Mixture		
12	Density		
13	Solubility		
14	Malleability		

Cut and Paste Pictures and Definitions

Use the internet or reference books to match up these definitons and pictures with the terms on the vocabulary page.

The ability of an object to float in water or air.	Allows electricity to flow through it easily.
A measure of how compact an object is.	The ability to be hammered or shaped under pressure without breaking.
solids, liquids, and gases	When 2 or more substances combine and a chemical change hasn't occurred.
The temperature at which the liquid freezes. Water freezes at 0° Celsius.	Attraction to a magnet.
Capable of being shaped or bent.	How much space an object takes up.
The degree of shininess of an object. Ex: bright or dull	Can be observed without chemically changing the matter.
The ability to be dissolved easily.	The resistance of a liquid to flow.

Printable of this page is available on resource page tinyurl.com/yc3bq2m3 (password: Matter).

Ooey Gooey Oobleck Lab

Name:

We are going to make and investigate the physical properties of Oobleck to see if it is a solid, liquid or a gas.

 Lab Safety

Goggles on! Tie hair back.
Do not eat Oobleck or leave it on carpets, furniture or other fabrics. To keep Oobleck in playing condition store it in a Ziploc bag in the refrigerator.

Background Research - List three properties of solids, liquids and gases:

Solids	Liquids	Gases

Materials:

Ziploc bag	Borax	Food Coloring	White Elmer's Glue
Warm Water	¼ and 1 Tablespoon	Spoon	1 Cup

Prepare Liquids:

1. Add 2 Tablespoons of warm water with 2 Tablespoons of Elmer's glue in your cup and stir until completely smooth. This is your white liquid.
2. Clean the Tablespoon and add 4 Tablespoons warm water and ¼ teaspoon of Borax to your bag. Seal bag and mix until the Borax is dissolved. This is your clear liquid.

Mix a White Liquid, a Clear Liquid and a Colored Liquid. What State will Oobleck be?

1. Open the plastic bag.
2. Choose and add 4 drops of the liquid food coloring.
3. Carefully pour the white liquid into the plastic bag.
4. Close the bag and knead the mixture well for 3 minutes.
5. Once 3 minutes have passed, take the Oobleck out of the bag and complete the investigation of its properties.

Investigation of Oobleck's Physical Properties:

1. Use your senses and measuring tools to identify the various physical properties of your Oobleck.
2. Record them in the table. Remember to use phrases such as "it smells like" and "it feels like."

Property	Observation	State of Matter
Example: Color	It looks green.	S L G
Length it Stretches		S L G
Bounce		S L G
Color		S L G
Smell		S L G
Texture		S L G
Shape		S L G
Ductility		S L G
Imprint Writing		S L G
Tear		S L G
Compress		S L G

Take Container Shape		S L G
Malleability		S L G
Viscosity high/low		S L G
Squeeze with fist		S L G
Keep shape when held for a minute		S L G

Conclusion:

From the data collected Oobleck appears to be a _____. (Solid, Liquid or Gas)

Questions:

1. What type of properties were identified in today's investigation? _____

2. Put a **star** by the properties identified through quantitative observations and an **X** by properties identified through qualitative observations.

3. If you measured the mass of your Oobleck, what unit would you use? _____ Would this observation be quantitative or qualitative? _____

4. What is Ductility? _____

5. If you put your Oobleck in the freezer overnight, would its ductility change? _____

6. When two or more elements are joined together with chemical bonds, they form a compound. On the other hand, when two or more elements are mixed together without chemical bonds, they form a mixture. Based on this information, is your Oobleck an element, a mixture, or a compound? _____

7. In the space provided, write a descriptive paragraph about your Oobleck using all the properties identified in this investigation.

Density Challenge Online Lab

Name:

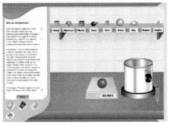

Go to: tinyurl.com/6ctnfr7

Density is a physical property of matter. It is how close the molecules of a substance are. Another way of saying this is how much mass an object has in a given space. What are two objects in your house that you think will sink in water and two you think will float?

1. Take the block of wood and place it on the scale. Mass is the amount of matter, or "stuff" in an object. What is the mass of the block of wood? Put a "g" (grams) after your number; this is the measurement unit used for mass.

2. Drop your block of wood into the tank of water. The number on the graduated cylinder gives the **volume**, the amount of space an object takes up. <u>What is the volume of your block of wood?</u> Put mL (milliliter) after your number. This or cm^3 is the measurement unit for volume. $1\ cm^3 = 1\ mL$

3. Hypothesize, or predict, whether your block of wood will float or sink in water and then watch what happens. Fill in the data table as you measure the rest of the objects on the screen.

This picture shows 4.9 mL

Material	Mass (g)	Volume (L)	Hypothesis (Sink or Float)	Result (sink or float?)
Wood	13.30 g	15.6 mL	Sink	float
Aluminum				
Plastic				
Lead				
Cork				
Steel				
Clay				
Rubber				
Don't measure the candle yet.				

Look at the data in your table.

4. Can you use just the mass to predict whether an object will sink or float?

5. Can you use just the volume of an object to predict whether it will sink or float?

6. Can you use mass **and** volume to predict whether an object will sink or float? Explain.

7. Measure just the mass and volume of the candle. **Mass:** _____ **Volume:** _____ Will it float or sink?

8. <u>Density</u> is the amount of mass in a specific volume. To find the density, divide the mass by the volume. The unit for density is g/cm^3. What is the density of a ball that has a mass of 6 grams and a volume of 2 cm^3? _____

9. Find the density of the following items from your data table and circle whether they sink or float:

   Wood _.85 g/cm^3_ sink / float **Aluminum** _____ sink / float **Plastic** _____ sink / float **Lead** _____ sink / float

10. The density of water is 1.0 g/mL or 1.0 g/cm^3. Use density to make a rule about whether an object will sink or float.

Physical Properties of Matter Project

There are so many cool physical properties and changes of matter to see. Make a presentation to show us all about these physical properties and their changes! Use printed resources or the internet to gather your information for this project. Instead of a quiz this week you will present your project.

You will find instructions for making a Prezi presentation below, but with permission you can make a poster, PowerPoint, or some other project instead. Your presentation needs to include:

- ☐ A title.
- ☐ Your first name.
- ☐ Description of what a physical property of matter is (in your own words).
- ☐ Insert a YouTube video on physical properties or changes. (If you are making a poster you can just use a picture).
- ☐ Description of 4 ways that physical properties are observed and measured.
- ☐ 5 types of physical properties, with a picture example of each.
- ☐ 3 examples of physical changes in real life, with a picture example of each.
- ☐ Spelling, grammar and creativity will be a part of your grade.

You can find this information by searching online. Some sites we recommend for good information are on our resource page tinyurl.com/ybuwjcnx (password: Matter). When you search make sure that you are using reputable sites. Ask sites and wiki sites are generally poor or unacceptable sources of information for a class project.

Making a 🌀 Prezi

Prezi is a really cool interactive slideshow that you can make for free. Here are the instructions to get you started!

1. Start by signing up for a **free "basic"** Prezi account: prezi.com/signup/basic
   a. **You will need an email address for this part.** You can use your parent's or your own email address.
2. We recommend watching the "getting started" Prezi video so that you can familiarize yourself with how to Prezi.
3. When you are ready, click on [New presentation] .
4. Browse through the templates until you find the one you like. Click on it then select "use this template."
5. Click on [Untitled Presentation] in the upper left to title your presentation.
6. Take a few minutes to explore your Prezi and to figure out where you want your topics to be placed.
   a. To zoom in, click on the slides to the left.
   b. Return to your big picture by clicking [◀] Overview or the return arrow [↩].
   c. Add new slides by clicking [+ Subtopic] or [+ Topic]
   d. Change the order of your slides by clicking on a slide and dragging it up and down the left hand column.
7. To write on a slide click on the slide and then click where you see text. You can add new text by clicking insert and choosing "insert text."
8. To insert a picture, click on insert and choose "insert picture." You will then choose a picture on your computer. Resize it by clicking on a corner and pulling it in or out. Then place the picture where you want it to go. You can use this tutorial on how to save images onto your computer: tinyurl.com/ycxbm2lr
9. To insert a video, first find a video on youtube that you like and copy the link (Ctrl+C or right click and copy). Then click on "insert," choose "insert video," and paste your link in the box (Ctrl+V or right click and paste).

Answer Key—Unit 7: Physical Properties and Changes

Physical Properties Cut and Paste

Physical Properties	Can be observed without chemically changing the matter.	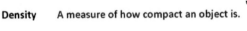
Viscosity	The resistance of a liquid to flow.	
Freezing Point	The temperature at which the liquid freezes. Water freezes at 0° C	
State of Matter	solids, liquids, and gases	
Luster	The degree of shininess of an object. Ex: bright or dull	
Ductility	Capable of being shaped or bent.	
Volume	How much space an object takes up.	Large Small
Buoyancy	The ability of an object to float in water or air.	
Conductor	Allows electricity to flow through easily.	
Magnetic	Attraction to a magnet.	
Mixture	When 2 or more substances combine and a chemical change hasn't occurred.	Trail Mix
Density	A measure of how compact an object is.	
Solubility	The ability to be dissolved easily.	Sugar
Malleability	The ability to be hammered or shaped under pressure without breaking.	

Ooey Gooey Oobleck Lab

Solid: Has a fixed shape and volume.
Liquid: Has no fixed shape but a fixed volume, can flow.
Gas: Has no fixed shape and no fixed volume.
Property Observations:
★Stretches: Far, measure with ruler
Bounce: slight bounce
Color: Will vary
Smell: Will vary
Texture: Smooth, sticky
Shape: Does not keep shape when held. When sitting on table it will keep its shape.
Ductility: Can be stretched
Imprint Writing: Similar to silly putty, it will pick up pencil writing and some pen.
Tear: Can be torn
Compress: Does not
Take Container Shape: Yes
Malleability: Can be hammered flat with a fist.
Conclusion: Students will choose either a solid or a liquid. Oobleck is actually a non-Newtonian fluid which means it sometimes acts as a solid and sometimes as a liquid. It is also a polymer and its molecules are arranged in a long chain that stretches.
1. Physical properties
2. Stretching is the only Quantitative (uses numbers) observation. The rest are Qualitative
3. Grams, Quantitative
4. Capable of being drawn out into a wire or thread.
5. Answers can vary but yes the ductility would change. Students should notice that the temperature of their hands does increase ductility and viscosity therefore making the oobleck colder could make it lose its ductility.
6. It is a mixture but answers will vary.
7. Students should use the properties they identified to write a descriptive paragraph.

Density Challenge Online Lab
1. 13.30 g
2. 15.6 mL

Material	Mass	Volume	Hypothesis	Result
Wood	13.30 g	15.6 mL	Sink	float
Aluminum	5.6 g	1.1 mL	Will vary	sink
Plastic	4.00 g	4.1 mL	Will vary	float
Lead	20.00 g	1.8 mL	Will vary	sink
Cork	4.00 g	8.1 mL	Will vary	float
Steel	8.30 g	1.7 mL	Will vary	sink
Clay	15.60 g	8.6 mL	Will vary	sink
Rubber	5.90 g	4.9 mL	Will vary	sink

4. No, some things with a big mass floated and other items with a small mass sank.
5. No, some items with a large volume sunk and others with a large volume floated.
6. Yes, if the mass is less than the volume it will float.
7. Mass: 10.50g Volume: 10.6 mL - Float
8. 3 g/cm^3
9. Wood: .85g/cm^3 Float; Aluminum: 5.09g/cm^3 Sink; Plastic .98g/cm^3 Float; Lead 11.11g/cm^3 Sink
10. If the density of an object is less than the density of water then it will float.

Rubric for Prezi Project
Subtract points if an item is incorrect, missing or only partially correct or if the writing is not in the student's own words.
Observed and Measured: Length, Temperature, Volume, Mass, Weight, Density, are all possible answers.
Types of Properties: Color, Lustre, Malleability, Ductility, Shape, Density, State, Conductor of Electricity and Magnetism are all possible answers.
Types of Changes: shape, volume, state, temperature, mixing, crushing.

Content - Physical Properties and Changes	Points Possible	Points Given
Description of Property	4	
Youtube Video	2	
Observed and Measured	4	
5 Types of Properties	5	
5 Picture Examples of Properties	5	
3 Examples of Changes	3	
3 Picture Examples of Changes	3	
Technical		
Title	1	
Student Name	1	
Spelling	3	
Grammar	3	
Creativity	8	
Quality	8	
Total Points	50	**/50**

Chemical Properties & Changes

Chemical Properties & Changes

This week students will learn that a chemical change actually changes the chemical identity of an element or molecule. Chemical properties can only be identified by changing a substance.

Keywords:

Chemical Properties	Properties	Reactants	Chemical Equation
Chemical Changes	Exothermic Reaction	Products	Balance
Chemical Reaction	Endothermic Reaction	Catalysts	

Day 1—Burning Steel Wool Demo + Cool Facts and Chemical Properties

Use the information at the top of "Cool Facts and Chemical Properties" to talk to students about what a chemical change is. Look at the clues that show whether or not a chemical change has occurred. Show students the burning steel wool demo and ask them if they think a chemical or physical change has occurred. Have students list clues they see to support their answers. Students will then complete the worksheet to identify if the fact contains a chemical property or change and/or a physical property or change.

Day 2—Crazy Elephant Toothpaste Lab

This is an easy and dramatic lab that really illustrates how the properties of a substance change in a chemical reaction. This chemical reaction is an exothermic reaction (energy released), so the foam 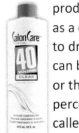 product will feel warm to the touch. The yeast in this lab acts as a catalyst to speed up the reaction that causes the hydrogen to dramatically decompose into water and oxygen gas. This lab can be done with 3% hydrogen peroxide you find at Walmart or the drugstore, BUT it is even cooler if you can get a higher percentage of hydrogen peroxide. We recommend a product called 20 Volume or 40 Volume Clear Developer (hydrogen peroxide). This can be found at beauty supply stores such as Sally's Beauty Supply. If you have time and enough materials, have students change a variable (type of peroxide, amount of yeast or soap) to see if that makes a difference in the foam produced by this reaction.

Day 3—Chemical Explosions and Changes

These two online labs let students see a variety of chemical reactions. In the first lab, "Chemical and Physical Change Examples," students identify whether they are seeing a chemical or a physical change taking place. This first lab does not work well in the browser google chrome, we found internet explorer and safari to work best with it. The second lab, "Physical Science Lab-Explosions," takes students into a laboratory where they get to test explosive chemical reactions and learn to balance simple chemical equations.

!Big !idea *Matter undergoes predictable chemical reactions. These reactions or changes, involve the rearrangement or reorganization of atoms.*

Day 4—Chemical Properties of Matter Prezi Project

Students are going to add to their physical properties prezi so that it also includes information about chemical reactions and changes. Doing this will force students to look at physical and chemical properties side by side so that they can more clearly see the differences between the two. Students will also try some new techniques as they work on this addition to their Prezi Project. Creating a presentation is a fantastic way for students to learn technology skills and an interesting way for them to learn. On our resource page tinyurl.com/ybuwjcnx (password: Matter), we have provided some great links for students to use as they research. Students can also search for the information on their own. Caution them away from sites that do not look professional, or any type of wiki or answer site. These are not reliable or accepted sources for a class project. A rubric, for grading, is included on the answer key page.

Materials:

- Pan or Tray to Catch Mess
- 20 oz Soda Bottle, empty
- 40 Volume Hydrogen Peroxide (8-15%) available at beauty supply stores. Drugstores carry 3% hydrogen peroxide; this will work too but with less effect.
- Fast Rising Yeast
- Dawn Dish Detergent
- Clear Cup
- Goggles
- Food Coloring
- Fine Steel Wool –Grades 00, 000 or 0000—no soap
- 9 Volt Battery or Lighter

Day 5—Finish Prezi Project and PRESENTATION

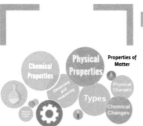

Students can take some time to finish their prezi and then present it for their quiz grade. This project covers chemical properties and changes and ties them into everyday life. This presentation incorporates technology into the unit. A rubric for grading is included on the answer key page.

Next Generation Science Standards—Unit 8

MS-PS1-1: Substances are made from different types of atoms, which combine with one another in various ways. Atoms form molecules that range in size from two to thousands of atoms.

MS-PS1-2: Analyze and interpret data on the properties of substances before and after the substances interact to determine if a chemical reaction has occurred.

MS-PS1-2; MS-PS1-3: Each pure substance has characteristic physical and chemical properties (for any bulk quantity under given conditions) that can be used to identify it.

MS-PS1-2; MS-PS1-3; MS-PS1-5: Substances react chemically in characteristic ways. In a chemical process, the atoms that make up the original substances are regrouped into different molecules, and these new substances have different properties from those of the reactants.

MS-PS1-3; MS-PS1-2 and MS-PS1-5: Substances react chemically in characteristic ways. In a chemical process, the atoms that make up the original substances are regrouped into different molecules, and these new substances have different properties from those of the reactants.

MS-PS1-4: The term "heat" as used in everyday language refers both to thermal energy (the motion of atoms or molecules within a substance) and the transfer of that thermal energy from one object to another. In science, heat is used only for this second meaning; it refers to the energy transferred due to the temperature difference between two objects.

MS-PS1-6: Some chemical reactions release energy, others store energy.

Burning Steel Wool Demo

A Chemical Change Demo

Materials:

- New 9 Volt Battery
- Fine Steel Wool without soap - Grade 00,000 or 0000
- Heat Proof Dish
- Heat Proof Surface or Pot Holder
- Goggles

Caution: This experiment involves fire and high heat. Wear safety glasses, use a heat proof container, and have water on hand in case you need to extinguish this small fire.

What to Do:

1. Allow students to feel and look at the piece of steel wool. Write down observations about it together.
2. Review signs of a chemical change with students: Unexpected Color Change, Change in Smell, Fire Produced, Gas Bubbles Appear, Electricity or Energy is Made, Light is Produced, Unexpected Temperature Change, Solid Forms from Liquids. Also remind students that a chemical change results in a new substance or substances.
3. Place a ball of steel wool (the size of a sponge) in your heat proof container, on a heat proof surface.
4. Hold the terminals of your 9 volt battery to the steel wool. The steel will begin to burn.
5. You can gently blow on the steel wool to spread the burning reaction.
6. Ask students to list the signs of a chemical change they witnessed, as the steel wool burned.
7. The container and steel wool will be hot, so do not touch them with your hands for at least 10 minutes. You can carefully look at the steel wool and prod it with a heat proof instrument once it has finished burning.
8. Look at the burned steel wool with the students. How is it different from before the burning reaction? (It should be a slightly different color, not as shiny and powdery.) Try to light it on fire again. Does it burn now? (It should not burn anymore.)
9. A chemical change changes the identity of a substance, resulting in something new and different. Ask students what properties of the burned steel wool are different from the original, proving that a true chemical change took place.

What Happened:

Steel wool is mostly iron. Iron wants to react with the oxygen, and heat is one way to speed up this reaction. The electrical current from the 9 volt battery heats up the fine strands of the steel wool enough for it to light on fire. This heat reaction causes the iron in your steel wool to react with the oxygen in the air creating iron oxide.

$$2Fe + 3O_2 \rightarrow 2Fe_2O_2$$

The combination of iron and oxygen is an oxidation reaction. Oxidation is a type of chemical reaction that takes place when a substance combines with oxygen. Rust or an apple browning in air are also examples of an oxidation reaction.

Cool Facts and Chemical Properties

Name:

Properties of Matter are the characteristics and behaviors we use to describe matter. There are two types of properties: **Chemical** and **Physical**.

Each substance has specific **properties** which help us to identify it and use it. For example Red food coloring has a red color (physical property) but it loses its color as it reacts with bleach (chemical property).

Chemical changes result in an entirely new substance. These changes are usually more obvious than a physical change. You cannot reverse a chemical change. Examples of a chemical change would be rusting and burning.

Clues that a chemical change have happened are:
- Unexpected color change
- Change in smell
- Fire is produced
- Gas bubbles appear
- Electricity or energy is made
- Light is produced
- Solid forms from liquids
- Unexpected temperature change

Write a "C" if the cool fact illustrates a chemical property or change and/or a "P" if it illustrates physical instead. Explain your choice in the line below each fact.

_____ 1. Exploding fireworks used to be only orange and white. In the Middle Ages new colors were made by burning different salts. The hardest color to create is blue.

_____ 2. Liquid mercury is so dense that you can float a coin in it.

_____ 3. A piece of toast was burned in the shape of the "Virgin Mary" and then sold for $28,000!

_____ 4. I picked up a metal chunk of the element Gallium and it melted from the heat of my hand.

_____ 5. You can make steel and iron rust in just 10 minutes. Soak it in vinegar for five minutes. Remove it, then cover the metal with salt and hydrogen peroxide for five minutes.

_____ 6. One inch of liquid rain is equal to 10 inches of frozen snow!

_____ 7. You can cut the metal potassium with a knife but when you drop it in water it will burst into flames!

_____ 8. With the right amount of pressure and heat, the graphite in your pencil will turn into a diamond!

_____ 9. Almost every day of his life, Albert Einstein fried up and ate two eggs.

_____ 10. A team of scientists in Georgia painted a picture of the Mona Lisa that is is a third the width of a human hair. It is the world's smallest painting!

_____ 11. If you chew a piece of a cracker in your mouth for a minute it will start to taste sweet. This is because the amylase in your saliva breaks down the cracker starch into sugars.

_____ 12. A handful of salt poured and mixed into water the makes the water level go down instead of up.

Crazy Elephant Toothpaste Lab

Name:

We are going to create a cool and surprising chemical reaction.

Lab Safety

Goggles on! Tie hair back.
Hydrogen peroxide can irritate skin and eyes and bleach clothes, it is important to wear goggles the entire time. This lab can be messy.

Background Info:

When a **chemical reaction** happens, energy is either released or absorbed. Energy is usually released as heat energy and the temperature will go up and feel warm or even extremely hot. This is an **exothermic reaction**. The opposite of an exothermic reaction is an endothermic reaction. In an **endothermic reaction,** energy is absorbed and the substance and surroundings will feel colder.

During a chemical reaction substances called **reactants** change into new substances called **products.** These new products have their own properties and might change volume, become a gas or turn a different color.

Chemists use **catalysts** in reactions. A catalyst will boost a reaction, making it happen more quickly. This happens because a catalyst either allows a reaction to happen with less energy, or it provides the energy needed for that reaction.

Materials:

40 Volume Hydrogen Peroxide (12%)	Rapid Rise or Active Yeast	Food Coloring	Dawn Dish Soap	20 oz Soda Bottle, empty
Casserole Dish or Tray	Tablespoon and ½ Cup	Cup	Very Warm Water	Dawn Dish Soap

1. Place your empty soda or water bottle in the center of your casserole dish or tray.
2. Pour a ½ cup of the hydrogen peroxide into the bottle.
3. Add 4-5 drops of food coloring into the bottle and a Tablespoon of the dish soap. Gently swirl the bottle to mix your ingredients.
4. Add 3 Tablespoons of very warm water to your cup. pour a packet of yeast into the cup and stir for 30 seconds (sing the alphabet) until there are no clumps in your solution.
5. Pour your yeast mixture into the soda bottle and watch what happens!
6. Feel the foam and the bottle. Would you describe the temperature as warm or cool?
7. Write down your observations. Measure the volume of the foam with a beaker or measuring cup, if you can, and include this in your observations.

Questions:

1. After the reaction, was the temperature of the bottle and the foam warm or cool? Would you say this was an endothermic or an exothermic reaction? Why?

2. The gas produced from the reactants in this chemical reaction is a _____? Which of the reactants would you say was responsible for this gas?

3. What is a catalyst? What do you think the catalyst was for this reaction? Why?

4. In this experiment hydrogen peroxide decomposes to form water and oxygen. Balance the chemical equation, as you learned how to do in the "Chemical Explosions and Changes" online lab:
$$2H_2O_2 \rightarrow \underline{\quad} H_2O + \underline{\quad} O_2$$

5. What is one variable you think could be changed to create more foam? If you tested this, the variable you change would be your _____ variable. What would be your dependent variable?
   Challenge: Run an experiment to test this.

Chemical Explosions and Changes

Name:

Chemical and Physical Change Examples

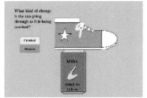

Go to: tinyurl.com/2ayogvz

(Note you might need to use a different browser. We found Internet Explorer or Safari to work well.)

Define each type of change:

Physical	Chemical

Complete the data table as you move through this lab:

Example	Type of Change	Explanation
Soda Can		
Penny		
Burning Tree		
Growing Plant		
Breaking Window		
Fireworks		
Baking Cake		
Water Freezing		
Ripped Paper		
Melting Snowman		
Baking Soda + Vinegar		
Boiling Water		

Physical Science Lab - Explosions

Go to: tinyurl.com/hsmfflh

Example	Observations:	Feedback	Type of Change
Sodium + Chlorine Gas			
Potassium iodide + Lead II Nitrate			
Ice Bomb			
Nitrogen Triiodide			

1. Which of the following statements best described why the reaction between sodium and chlorine is not useful in fireworks?

Balancing Chemical Equations

Enter the numbers for each molecule that balanced your Equation, below:

2. _____ H_2 + _____ O_2 = _____ H_2O
   Hydrogen + Oxygen = Water

3. _____ N_2 + _____ H_2 = _____ NH_3
   Nitrogen + Hydrogen = Ammonia

4. _____ Na + _____ Cl_2 = _____ NaCl
   Sodium + Chlorine = Sodium Chloride
   (white solid)

5. _____ KI + _____ $Pb(NO_3)_2$ = _____ KNO_3 + _____ PbI_2
   Potassium + Lead (II) = Potassium + Lead iodide
   iodide nitrate nitrate (yellow precipitate)

Chemical Properties of Matter Project
Part 2

There are so many cool chemical properties and changes of matter to see. Show us about chemical properties and their changes by adding them to the physical properties project you did in the last unit. Instead of a quiz this week, you will present your project.

You will find instructions for adding onto your Prezi presentation below. With permission you can add onto some other project, such as a poster or PowerPoint. Your presentation needs to include:

- ☐ "Properties of Matter" title.
- ☐ Description of what a chemical property of matter is (in your own words).
- ☐ Insert a YouTube video on chemical properties or changes. (If you are making a poster you can just use a picture).
- ☐ Description of ways that chemical properties are observed and measured.
- ☐ 3 types of chemical properties, with a picture example of each.
- ☐ 3 examples of chemical changes in real life, with a picture example of each.
- ☐ 8 clues of a chemical change, with a picture example of each
- ☐ State somewhere, what you think makes a chemical change different from a physical change.
- ☐ Spelling, grammar and creativity will be a part of your grade.

You can find this information by searching online. Some sites we recommend for good information are on the resource page tinyurl.com/ybuwjcnx (password: Matter). When you search make sure that you are using reputable sites. Ask sites and wiki sites are generally poor or unacceptable sources of information for a class project.

Making a 🔘 Prezi -Part 2

Try some of these new tips and tricks to make your Prezi even better!

1. Click [+ Topic] and then Stack [TITLE] to add extra big topic slides to your presentation.
2. Add new text by clicking insert and choosing "insert text."
3. Click on any text and you will see that you can change the font, size and color and even add bullets.

4. Try rotating your content:

5. Click on any object and add an animation to it.
   a. You can choose "Fade in" or fade out to make objects and text appear and disappear during your presentation.
   b. You can also choose a "Zoom" to zoom into or out of an area during your presentation.
      Tip: to adjust the zoom area just change the size of the rectangle that appears when you choose to zoom.

Chemical Explosions and Changes

1: Chemical and Physical Change Examples

Chemical Change Definition: any new substance formed with different chemical properties than the original substance.

Physical Change Definition: the chemical properties of a substance stay the same, but the state, shape, and/or size of the substance change.

Example	Type	Explanation
Soda Can	Physical	Only its shape is changed.
Penny	Chemical	Salt and vinegar cause a chemical reaction in the penny
Burning Tree	Chemical	Ash and Carbon are new substances that are produced
Growing Plant	Chemical	Sunlight creates food from a chemical reaction to help the plant grow.
Breaking Window	Physical	There is only a change in size and shape. Glass is still glass.
Fireworks	Chemical	An explosion is a chemical change.
Baking Cake	Chemical	A new substance is created and cannot be split into separate substances again.
Water Freezing	Physical	This is a change of state.
Ripped Paper	Physical	Only the size is changed.
Melting Snowman	Physical	Ice to water is a change of state.
Baking Soda + Vinegar	Chemical	Mixing baking soda and vinegar causes a chemical reaction.
Boiling Water	Physical	Water to gas is just a change of state.

2: Physical Science Lab-Explosions

Example	Observations:	Feedback	Type
Sodium, Chlorine Gas	Color Change, Formation of Solid, Energy Change	White, crystalline solid forms + energy released.	Chemical
Potassium iodide + Lead (II) Nitrate	Color Change, Formation of Solid	A yellow precipitate forms.	Chemical
Ice Bomb	Formation of Solid, Change in Energy	Energy was removed and a solid formed.	Physical
Nitrogen Triiodide	Color Change, Formation of Gas, Energy Change	Purple gas, iodine, produced + a change in energy.	Chemical

1. Poisonous gas is one of the reactants.
2. 2, 1, 2
3. 1, 3, 2
4. 2, 1, 2
5. 2, 1, 2, 1

Crazy Elephant Toothpaste Lab

1. The bottle and the foam should be warm to very warm. Even though warm water was used with the yeast the foam will be even warmer than that. Heat energy was released, which is why you feel the warmth. This is an exothermic reaction.
2. Product; Answers will vary as students guess which reactant or reactants is responsible for the gas produced in this experiment. What really happened is the hydrogen peroxide decomposed into water and oxygen gas.
3. A catalyst boosts a reaction making it happen more quickly. Answers will vary as students guess which is the catalyst. The yeast is the true catalyst in this reaction. Yeast's enzyme catalase is what speeds up the reaction.

Cool Facts and Chemical Properties

4. $\underline{2}\ H_2O + \underline{1}\ O_2$
5. Answers will vary as students choose the variable they would want to test.

Cool Facts and Chemical Properties

1. C ; Exploding the salts and chemicals generates heat, different colors and light.
2. P ; Density and Floating (Buoyancy) are both physical properties that do not change a substance.
3. C ; Burning toast changes its color and generates a smell.
4. P ; Changing state is a physical change
5. C ; Rusting changes the color.
6. P ; Volume and state change are physical changes
7. C, P ; Cutting is a physical change but a reaction that generates fire is a chemical change
8. P ; Pressure causes a physical change. It is just pushing the same atoms or molecules closer together.
9. C ; Frying an egg changes it. You see a color change and there is a smell
10. P ; Painting is a physical change. No new substance is formed.
11. P, C ; Chewing is a physical change. Amylase breaking down starch into sugars is a chemical change.
12. P ; Salt mixing with water into a solution is a physical change.

Rubric for Prezi Project

Subtract points if an item is incorrect, missing or only partially correct or if the writing is not in the student's own words.

Observed and Measured: Can only be observed and measured by changing the substance's identity. We can measure color of light produced, flammability, etc

Types of Properties: Flammability, pH, Reactivity, Toxicity, Heat of Combustion, Oxidation

Types of Changes: rust, baking cake, something on fire, a chemical reaction, etc.

Clues of Change: color change, gas bubbles appear, formation of a solid, temperature change, light, change in smell, change in taste, volume change, electricity made, fire produced

Content - Chemical Properties and Changes	Points Possible	Points Given
Description of Property	4	
Youtube Video	2	
Observed and Measured	3	
3 Types of Properties	3	
3 Picture Examples of Properties	3	
3 Examples of Changes	3	
3 Picture Examples of Changes	3	
8 Chemical Change Clues (.5 each)	4	
8 Picture Examples of Clues (.5 each)	4	
Technical		
Title "Property of Matter"	1	
Spelling	3	
Grammar	3	
Creativity	6	
Quality	8	
Total Points	50	/50

Acids & Bases

Acids & Bases

This week students will learn about acids, bases and neutrals. They will use an indicator to identify acids, bases and neutrals in their everyday life.

Keywords:

Acids	Neutral	Ph	Hydrogen ion (H+)
Bases	Indicator	Acid Rain	Hydroxide ions (OH-)
Acid Rain			

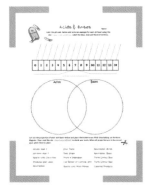

Day 1—Drinkable Acid Demo + Acids and Bases

In this hands-on intro activity students will color the pH scale and learn everyday examples of each level of the pH scale. Before reading the article, students will cut out the facts and anticipate where they go on the venn diagram. They will check their work as they read the article. Once all items are placed correctly students will tape or paste them in place.

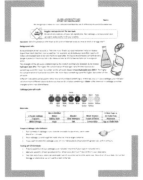

Day 2—Acid Attack Lab

Students will make their own indicator out of purple cabbage. Making an indicator out of cabbage really brings the idea of acids and bases home to students. Students will test different household substances to see which are acids and bases and what they have in common. You can definitely stray from the materials list on this lab or add to it. Test items you are curious about to see if they are an acid or a base. You should still test vinegar though because students will need it for the second part of the lab. In the second part of the lab students should have found that vinegar is the strongest acid they tested and use it with their egg or chalk. It will take a day or two, but the vinegar will eat away the chalk or the egg shell. Students will see bubbles around the egg shell or chalk as the chemical reaction is slowly taking place between the acid and the calcium carbonate that makes up the egg shell and chalk.

Cabbage Juice Ph Scale:

Acid	Acid	Acid	Acid-Neutral	Base	Base	Base	Base
0-1	2-3	4-5	6-7	8	9-10	11-13	14
Red	Light Pink	Dark Pink	Purple	Blue	Blue-Green	Green-Yellow	Yellow

!Big !idea

Acids and bases are found in foods, plants, products and in our bodies. They can be classified as acids, bases or neutrals, and are identified with indicators.

Day 3—Alien Juice Bar

This is a favorite online lab for so many students. The first part of this lab has students identifying acids and bases. In the second part of the lab the students need to correctly find acids and bases by their pH level and must correctly give them to an alien customer. In the third part of this lab students will use different ingredients to make acids (6.9 or lower), bases (8.0 or higher) or neutrals (7.0-7.9). At the end of this online lab students will have a clear understanding of which pH levels are acids, which are bases and which are neutrals.

Materials:

- Purple Cabbage
- Clear Shampoo
- Lemon Juice
- Ammonia
- Baking Soda
- Cream of Tartar
- Lemon Juice
- Sugar
- White Vinegar
- Salt
- Baking Soda
- Frozen Grape or Cranberry Juice Concentrate
- Ice Cube Tray, Egg Carton or 9 Clear Cups
- Egg or Chalk Stick (not dustless-must contain calcium carbonate)
- Mesh Strainer
- Goggles
- Blender
- 2 Lemons

Day 4—Color Chemistry Review

A coloring review like this engages students and helps them to review or learn in an entertaining way. Something like this is fun and catches students attention because they do not get to "color" in school at their age. This is the last unit of this chemistry book and this activity covers all of the nine units. In this activity students will match by coloring the parts of the picture that have to do with each topic.

Day 5—QUIZ: Acids and Bases

This is a culmination of the week's learning activities. You can have students study their class work. The quiz will cover the difference between acids and bases and their properties. Students should be able to identify acids and bases by their properties. Students should pay special attention to the terms in bold. The vocabulary list in your guide can also help them to prepare. The student notebook does not have a copy of the quiz so you will want to make sure you have the quiz ready for them to take.

Next Generation Science Standards—Unit 9

MS-PS1-2: Analyze and interpret data on the properties of substances before and after the substances interact to determine if a chemical reaction has occurred.

PS1.A: Structure and Properties of Matter-Each pure substance has characteristic physical and chemical properties (for any bulk quantity under given conditions) that can be used to identify it.

PS1.B: Chemical Reactions-Substances react chemically in characteristic ways. In a chemical process, the atoms that make up the original substances are regrouped into different molecules, and these new substances have different properties from those of the reactants.

Scientific Knowledge is Based on Empirical Evidence: Science knowledge is based upon logical and conceptual connections between evidence and explanations.

Fizzy Drinkable Acid

An Acid and Base Demo

You can drink this delicious demo. Make sure to use clean glassware and avoid getting lemon juice in your eyes. This demo makes one glass. Increase the amount of ingredients to make more.

What to Do:

1. Squeeze both lemons into your glass. Try to squeeze as much juice out of each lemon as possible.
2. Pour in an equal amount of cold water into your cup.
3. Stir in a teaspoon of baking soda. What does it do?
4. Stir in the sugar to sweeten this homemade lemonade and add ice.
5. Allow student to taste this drinkable acid. If you have more than one student you can small amounts into separate cups.

What Happened:

Lemon juice is an acid and baking soda is a base. When you add the two together the acid and the base chemically react. This reaction gives off carbon dioxide, which produces the bubbles. You can experiment with adding more baking soda to get the fizziness just right.

Materials:

- 2 Lemons
- Cold Water
- Baking Soda
- Sugar
- Glass
- Spoon
- Ice

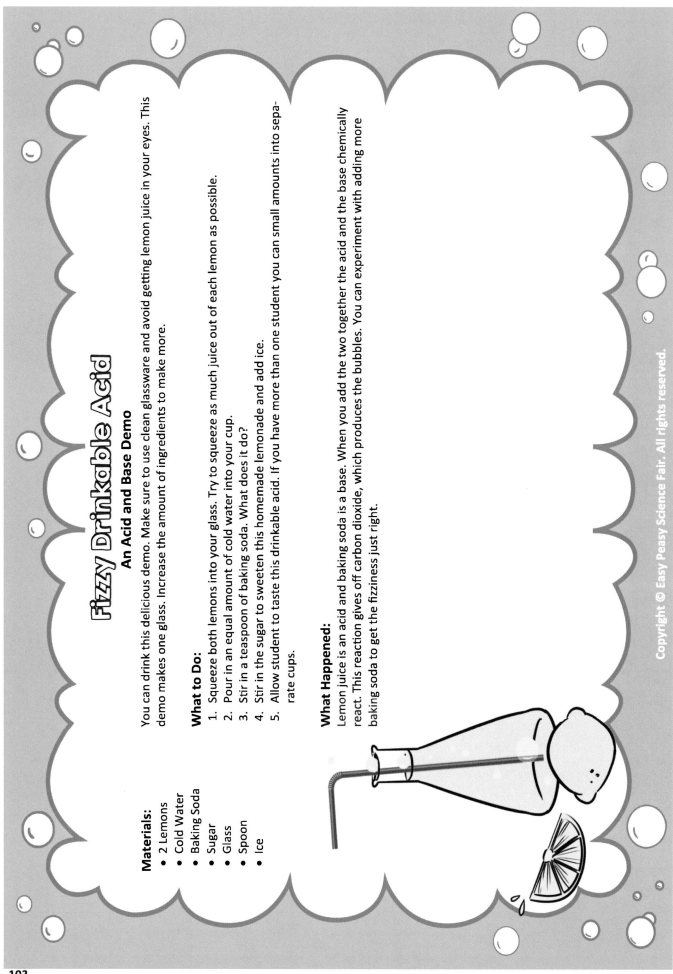

Acids & Bases

Name:

Color the pH scale below and write an example for each pH level using this site: tinyurl.com/yb38mxwj. **Label the Base, Acid and Neutral Sections.**

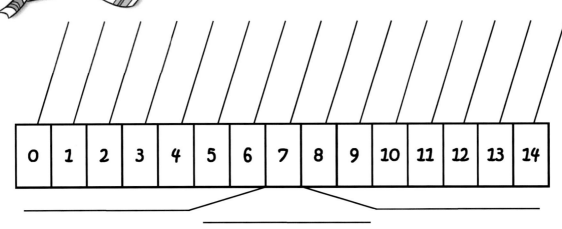

0	1	2	3	4	5	6	7	8	9	10	11	12	13	14

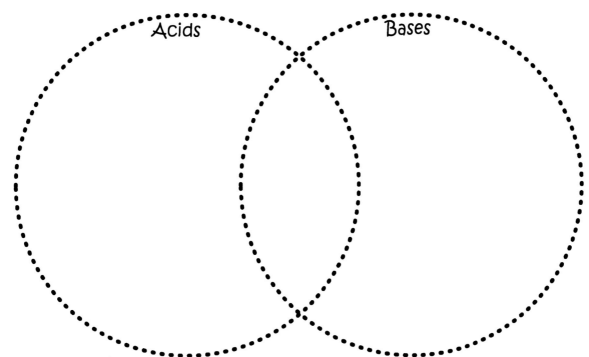

Acids

Bases

Cut out the properties of acids and bases below and place them where you think they belong on the Venn Diagram. Then read this site: tinyurl.com/cf456ef to check your work. When all properties are in the correct spot, paste them in place.

- -

pH less than 7	Sour Taste	Neutralizes Acids
pH more than 7	Feels Soapy	Neutralizes Bases
Reacts with Oils & Fats	Fruits & Vegetables	Turns Litmus Blue
Produces Salt when Neutralized	Can Blister or Corrode Skin	Turns Litmus Red
	Reacts with Most Metals	Cleaning Products

Acid Attack Lab

Name:

We are going to make our own indicator and test the pH of difference household substances.

Question: Which substance is the most acidic and will best eat away a piece of chalk or an egg shell?

Background Info:

Acids and bases are all around us. They are in our foods, our pools and even help our bodies digest food. Each has their own properties. For example, acids taste sour and often react with metals while bases taste bitter and have a slippery feel. Strong acids and bases can both be very dangerous and will burn your skin. We measure how acidic or basic a chemical is using a pH scale.

The strength of the pH scale is determined by the kind of ions that are released. Acids release **hydrogen ions (H+)**. The higher the concentration of hydrogen ions (H+) the more acidic something is and the lower its number on the pH scale. Bases release **hydroxide ions (OH-)**. The higher the concentration of hydroxide ions (OH-) the more basic something is and the higher its number on the pH scale.

Different indicators can be used to show how acidic or basic something is. In this lab, you will use a cabbage juice indicator which will turn different colors to show you how acidic or basic something is. **Flavin** is the chemical in cabbage juice that changes colors in acids and bases.

Cabbage juice pH scale:

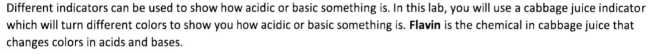

Acid	Acid	Acid	Acid-Neutral	Base	Base	Base	Base
0-1	2-3	4-5	6-7	8	9-10	11-13	14
Red	Light Pink	Dark Pink	Purple	Blue	Blue-Green	Green-Yellow	Yellow

Materials:

¼ Purple Cabbage	Warm Distilled Water	Blender	Mesh Strainer	9 Clear Cups, Ice Cube Tray or White Egg Carton
2 Spoons	Baking Soda	Clear Shampoo	Cream of Tartar	Ammonia
White Vinegar	Sugar	Salt	Lemon Juice	Egg or Chalk Stick

Prepare Cabbage Juice Indicator:

1. Put ¼ a head of cabbage in your blender and add 4 cups of very warm water. Blend for 1 minute.

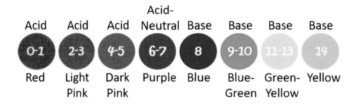

2. Pour cabbage juice through the mesh strainer into a larger container.
3. If you want to store the cabbage juice, stir in 2 Tablespoons of salt and refrigerate. Use within 24 hours.

Testing pH of Chemicals:

1. Place 2 spoonfuls of your cabbage juice indicator into one of your cups or ice cube wells.
2. Add one spoonful of baking soda and mix. What color did it turn? Record this in your data table.
3. Test the rest of your chemicals and water (which is a chemical too) the same way. Record all of your data. Do not test the egg or chalk stick, we will use this later in the lab.

Chemical	Cabbage Juice Color After	Conclusion: Acid, Base, Neutral	Ph #

4. Sort your results into the following categories. Underline what you believe to be your strongest acid and your strongest base.

Strong Acids	Weak Acids	Neutral	Weak Bases	Strong Bases

Acid Attack:

5. Place your egg or stick of chalk in a cup. Eggshells and chalk are made of **calcium carbonate**.

6. Pick the strongest acid you tested and pour it into the cup so that the egg is fully covered or so that half of the stick of chalk is in the strong acid.

7. Write down your observations after 10 minutes. Keep your egg or chalk in the acid for 2-3 days and then write down your final observations.

Observations after 10 Minutes	Observations after 2-3 Days

Neutralization: Is the color change from your cabbage juice reversible?

8. Add one of your colored basic chemicals (avoid baking soda - it can get messy) to a colored acid. See if you can get the color back to purple. Were you able to do it? _____ Yes _____ No

Questions:

1. Which of the chemicals you tested has the highest concentration of hydrogen ions (H+)?

2. What type of substance changes color when exposed to an acid or a base?

3. Milk has a pH of 6.8. Is it slightly acidic or slightly basic?

4. The burning of coal and fossil fuels release gases in the air that make our rain slightly acidic. This is called acid rain. What might acid rain do to buildings and statues made of limestone and marble which contain calcium carbonate, just like egg shells and chalk?

Alien Juice Bar

tinyurl.com/oqp7lka

Name:

Click on the link above. You will need Adobe Flash Player for this GEMS science activity. If you have trouble loading this lab try using a different browser. We found Internet Explorer or Safari to work well.

Challenge 1: Alien Juice Bar

- Click on **Challenge 1** and then **Start**.
- Add cabbage juice indicator to the drinks and write down what color they turn.
- Place the drinks on the shelf that you think they belong on. Hit "check me" when you think you have it right. Fill in the data table when you get the bottles all right.

Drink	Acid, Base or Neutral?	Color with Indicator

Click on "Test More," add the indicator to each drink and correctly sort them on the shelves. List the drinks correctly in the data table below.

Acid	Neutral	Base

Challenge 2: The Flying Cabbage Juice Bar

- Go to the **Main Menu** and choose **Challenge 2** and then **Start**.
- Your customer will ask for an acidic, neutral or basic drink. Pour the cabbage juice indicator into the bottles of "juice" to figure out if they are acidic, basic or neutral.
- When you find what your customer wants, pour it into their cup and they will drink it. Be careful! If you give your customer the wrong drink, they will get sick. If they get the wrong drink a second time, they die! Fill in the data table below as you go.

	Drink Wanted	Type of "Juice" you gave.	Yummy or Sick?	Yummy or Dead?
Alien 1				
Alien 2				
Alien 3				
Alien 4				
Alien 5				
Alien 6				

Challenge 3: Alien Juice Bar

- Go to the **Main Menu** and choose **Challenge 3** and then **Start**.
- Put cabbage juice indicator into each of the cups. Add the different juices to make the cups acidic, basic or neutral. Fill in the data tables as you go.
- When all of your cups are the correct pH level, the game will automatically move on.

Acidic

Starting pH #						
Starting Color						
Ending pH #						
Ending Color						

Basic

Starting pH #						
Starting Color						
Ending pH #						
Ending Color						

Neutral:

Hint: This is a tough one! Different juices will raise or lower the pH in different amounts. Figure out the right combinations and you will be able to get your pH to the correct levels.

Starting pH #						
Starting Color						
Ending pH #						
Ending Color						

Questions:

1. What is pH?

2. Put a square around the pH number/s that are neutral, a circle around the numbers that are acidic and a line under the numbers that are basic.

    0   1   2   3   4   5   6   7   8   9   10   11   12   13   14

3. How would you define an indicator? Does an indicator just have to be for acids and bases?

4. When you are making an acid a base or a base an acid, this is a chemical reaction. It is called a neutralization reaction. What signs of a chemical change do you see as an acid or a base is neutralized?

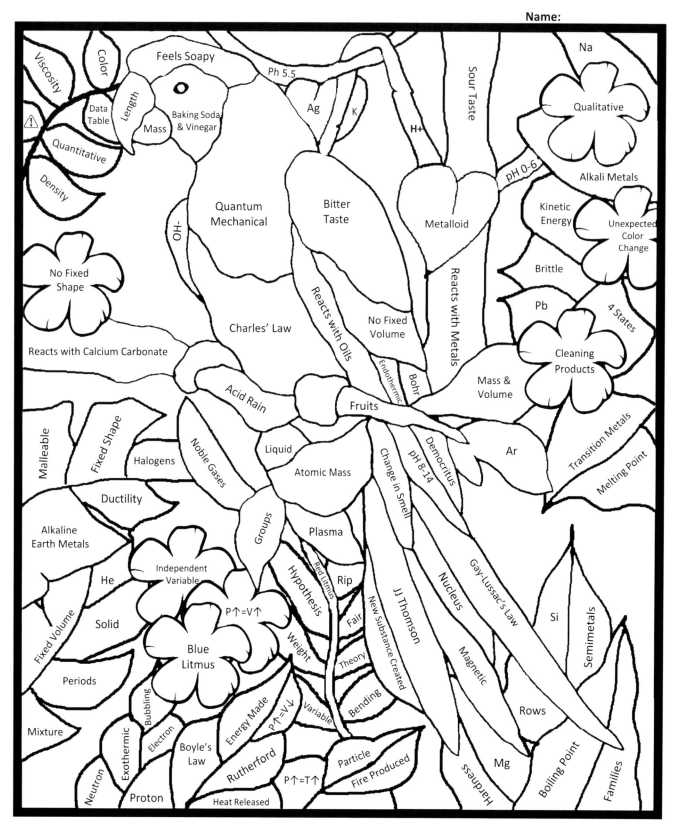

Color Chemistry Review

To find the color of each space, match it with the topic it best belongs to.

Bases-Dark Blue
Matter and its States-Light Green
Chemical Change-Light Blue

Gases-Purple
Atoms-Red
Acids-Brown

Physical Property-Yellow
Periodic Table-Green
Scientific Method and Safety-Orange

Invisible Ink Activity

An Acid Base Activity

Materials:

- Baking Soda
- Paper
- Water
- Paintbrush or Cotton Swab
- Frozen Grape Juice Concentrate

Caution: The grape juice concentrate can stain, so make sure that you do not get it on clothes. This makes a non-toxic invisible ink using baking soda (sodium bicarbonate).

What to Do:

1. Mix 1/4 cup baking soda with 1/4 cup of water in a cup or bowl.
2. Use a paintbrush or cotton swab to paint your secret message on a piece of paper.
3. Let this completely dry.
4. Use your paintbrush to paint grape juice concentrate across the paper. This will reveal your secret message!

What Happened:

Grape juice is an acid and it reacts with the baking soda which is a base. This reaction produces a different color so that your message is revealed.

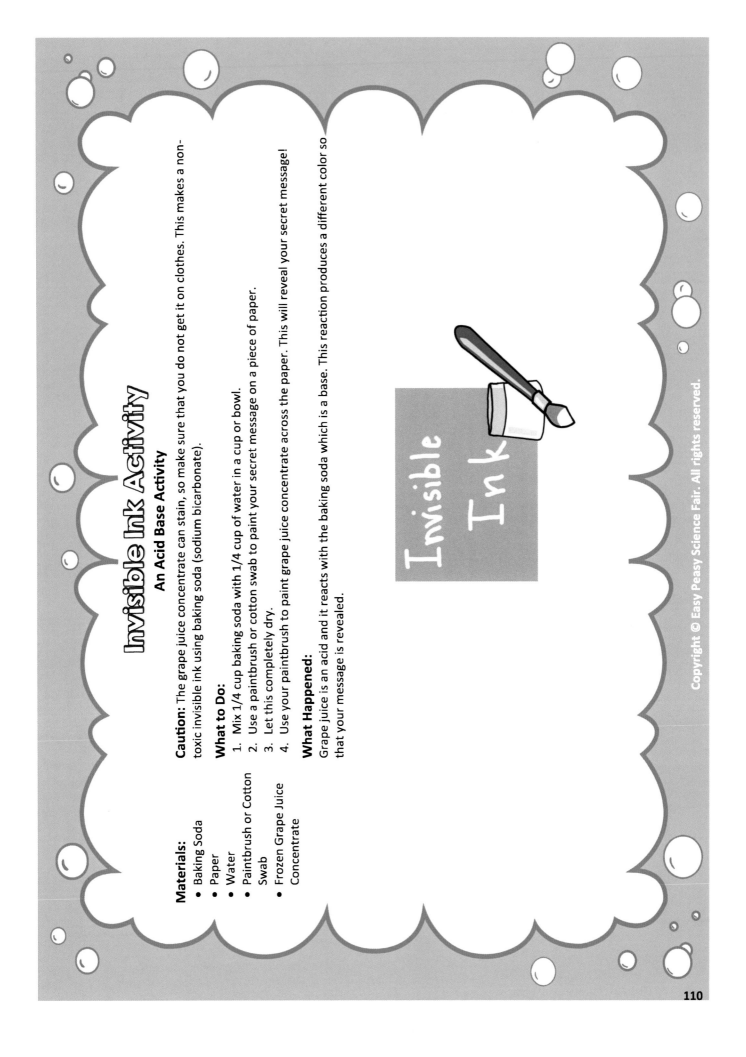

Invisible Ink

Acids and Bases Quiz

Multiple Choice

Identify the choice that best completes the statement or answers the question.

_____ 1. One way to identify acidic foods is because they taste _____.

    a. bitter   b. salty   c. sweet   d. sour

_____ 2. Acids have a pH that is _____.

    a. greater than 7   b. a color not a number   c. less than 7   d. equal to 7

_____ 3. Derek's drink has a pH of 7.5. This means that his drink is _____.

    a. weakly an acid   b. neutral   c. weakly a base   d. a strong acid

_____ 4. Patrick spilled a bottle of syrup on the floor. What should he use to clean it up with?

    a. acid   b. a neutral substance   c. litmus   d. base

_____ 5. The pH of pure water is _____.

    a. Acidic   b. Basic   c. Neutral   d. None of the above

_____ 6. Which of these chemicals has the highest nmber of hydroxide ions (OH-)?

    a. vinegar   b. hand soap   c. salt water   d. lemon juice

_____ 7. What type of substance changes color when exposed to an acid or a base?

    a. pH scale   b. neutral   c. indicator   d. alkali

_____ 8. The acid rain in New York city is damaging some beautiful statues and buildings. What is the cause of this acid rain?

    a. soil pollution   b. water pollution   c. air pollution   d. noise pollution

_____ 9. Dan wanted to neutralize a base. To do this he should _____.

    a. use an indicator   b. add an acid to it   c. add a base to it.   d. add water to it

_____ 10. This hazard symbol applies to

    a. neither acids or bases.   b. both acids and bases.   c. bases.   d. acids.

_____ 11. Jeanette pours a mystery liquid into her drink and the pH increases. The mystery liquid is _____.

    a. basic   b. solvent   c. sweet   d. acidic

_____ 12. Kara tastes a base. It probably tastes _____.

    a. Salty   b. Sweet   c. Spicy   d. Bitter

_____ 13. Cindy needs to find the liquid in her fridge with the lowest pH. Which one should she pick?

    a. salt water   b. pure water   c. milk   d. lemon juice

_____ 14. _____ is a scale of the acidity of a substance.

    a. indicator   b. litmus   c. pH   d. alkali

_____ 15. When an indicator changes color in an acid or a base, this is a _____.

    a. physical change   b. state change   c. chemical change   d. Biological change

Answer Key—Unit 9: Acids and Bases

Acids and Bases

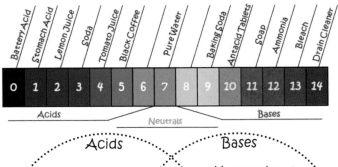

Acids
- pH less than 7
- Sour Taste
- Fruits & Vegetables
- Neutralizes Bases
- Turns Litmus Red
- Reacts with Most Metals

(Overlap) - Produces Salt when Neutralized - Can Blister & Corrode

Bases
- pH more than 7
- Reacts with Oils & Fats
- Feels Soapy
- Neutralizes Acids
- Turns Litmus Blue
- Cleaning Products

Acid Attack Lab

Distilled Water: Purple, Neutral, 6-7
Baking Soda: Blue, Base, 8
Clear Shampoo: Blue-Green, Base, 10
Cream of Tartar: Dark Pink, Acid, 5
Ammonia: Green-Yellow, Base, 11
White Vinegar: Light Pink, Acid, 2-3
Sugar: Blue-Green, Base, 9
Salt: Blue, Base, 7
Lemon Juice: Dark/Light Pink, Acid, 4
Strong Acids: White Vinegar, Lemon Juice
Weak Acids: Cream of Tartar,
Neutral: Distilled Water
Weak Bases: Baking Soda, Salt, Sugar
Strong Bases: Ammonia, Shampoo
Observation after 10 Minutes: There should be bubbles all around the chalk or egg shell.
Observations after 2-3 Days: The egg shell will be completely eaten away and you will be able to see the egg sac which holds the yolk and white of the egg. The part of the chalk that was in the vinegar will be completely eaten away.
1. The strongest acid, <u>vinegar</u>, has the most hydrogen ions.
2. An indicator
3. Slightly acidic
4. These buildings and statues would be eaten away by the acid just like the egg or chalk were eaten away by the vinegar.

Alien Juice Bar

Challenge 1: Alien Juice Bar
Lemon Juice: Acid, Pink
Window Cleaner: Base, Green
Water: Neutral, Purple
<u>Acids:</u> Coffee, Orange Juice, Soda Pop, Tea
<u>Neutral:</u> Water
<u>Base:</u> Mouthwash, Cough Medicine, Liquid Soap, Toothpaste Juice
Challenge 2: The Flying Cabbage Juice Bar
Answers will vary
Challenge 3: Alien Juice Bar
Acidic:
<u>Starting Ph:</u> Answers will vary all should be above 7
<u>Starting Color:</u> Green
<u>Ending pH#:</u> Less than 7
<u>Ending Color:</u> Pink

Challenge 3: Alien Juice Bar

Basic:
<u>Starting Ph:</u> Answers will vary all should be below 7
<u>Starting Color:</u> Pink
<u>Ending pH#:</u> More than 7
<u>Ending Color:</u> Green

Neutral:
<u>Starting Ph:</u> Answers will vary none should be 7
<u>Starting Color:</u> Green and Pink
<u>Ending pH#:</u> 7-Slightly higher or lower
<u>Ending Color:</u> Purple

1. Measure of how acidic or basic something is.
2. (0 1 2 3 4 5 6) [7] 8 9 10 11 12 13 14
3. An indicator is something that reacts to show how acidic or basic something is. Different indicators could show other properties of a substance.
4. You see an unexpected color change.

Color Chemistry Review

Atoms	Chemical Change
Bohr	New Substance Created
Rutherford	Change in Smell
Electron	Heat Released
Proton	Bubbling
Neutron	Fire Produced
JJ Thomson	Unexpected Color Change
Democritus	Energy Made
Quantum Mechanical	Baking Soda & Vinegar
Nucleus	Exothermic
Particle	Endothermic

Gases	Matter & States	Periodic Table	Physical Property
Gay-Lussac's Law	Solid	Periods	Mixture
Charles' Law	Liquid	Groups	Bending
Boyle's Law	Plasma	Atomic Mass	Magnetic
No Fixed Shape	4 States	Families	Rip
No Fixed Volume	Fixed Shape	Rows	Boiling Point
P↑=V↓	Fixed Volume	He	Color
P↑=V↑	Mass & Volume	Ar	Density
P↑=T↑	Kinetic Energy	Na	Mass
		K	Malleable

Scientific Method	Acids	Mg	Ductility
Variable	Sour Taste	Pb	Hardness
Data Table	H+	Ag	Length
Fair	pH 0-6	Si	Weight
Independent Variable	Reacts w/ Calcium	Alkaline Earth Metals	Melting Point
Quantitative	Reacts w/ Metals	Transition Metals	Brittle
Qualitative	Acid Rain	Noble Gases	Viscosity
Theory	Fruits	Semimetals	
Hypothesis	Red Litmus	Halogens	**Bases**
⚠	pH 5.5	Metalloid	Bitter Taste
		Alkali Metals	OH-

Bases
pH 8-14
Feels Soapy
Reacts with Oils
Cleaning Products
Blue Litmus

Acids and Bases Quiz

1. D
2. C
3. C
4. D
5. C
6. B
7. C
8. C
9. B
10. B
11. A
12. D
13. D
14. C
15. C

→

Materials

Full Materials List for the entire unit.

Item	Amount Needed	Amount per Group of 20	Type	Labs
60 ml Syringe	1	4	Tool	Gas Station Labs
Casserole dish or plate with lip	1	3	Tool	Gas Station Labs
Disposable Pie or Casserole Tin	1	10	Tool	Rainbow Flame Lab
Glass dish or disposable pie pan	1		Tool	Melting Styrofoam Cup Demo
Goggles	1	20	Tool	All Labs
Heat Source	1	10	Tool	Melting Ice Lab
Lighter or Match	1	5	Tool	Rainbow Flame Lab, Burning Dollar Demo
Magnifying Glass or Pocket Microscope	1	5	Tool	Mentos and Diet Coke
Measuring Spoons	1	5	Tool	Oobleck Physical Properties, Fake Blood Lab
Measuring Tape	1	5	Tool	Mentos and Diet Coke
Pan or Tray to Catch Mess	1	10	Tool	Elephant Toothpaste Lab
Spoon	2	20	Tool	Fake Blood Lab, Acid Attack Lab
Strainer	1	1	Tool	Acid Attack Lab
Thermometer 0°C- 100°C or 30°F-212°F	1	10	Tool	Melting Ice Lab
Timer (can use phone)	1	10	Tool	Melting Ice Lab
Tongs	1		Tool	Burning Money Demo
2-Liter Bottle, empty	1	3	Dry	Gas Station Labs
Balloon	1	3	Dry	Gas Station Labs
Clear Cup	5	50	Dry	Melting Ice Lab, Mentos and Diet Coke, Oobleck Physical Properties, Elephant Toothpaste Lab
Dry Erase Marker	1	20	Dry	Periodic Table Battleship
Empty Soda Bottle, empty	1	10	Dry	Elephant Toothpaste Lab
File or Regular Folder	1	20	Dry	Periodic Table Battleship
Laminated Periodic Tables or use page protectors instead of laminating.	2 copies	40	Dry	Periodic Table Battleship
Pot holder or Small Towel	1	10	Dry	Rainbow Flame Lab
Styrofoam Cup	1		Dry	Melting Styrofoam Cup Demo
Tape	2 strips	1-2 rolls	Dry	Periodic Table Battleship
Ziploc, sandwich or quart	2	40	Dry	Fake Blood Lab, Oobleck Physical Properties
40 Volume Hydrogen Peroxide (8-15%) Available at beauty supply stores; Drugstores carry 3% hydrogen peroxide, this will work too but with less effect.	1/2 cup	5 cups		Elephant Toothpaste Lab
70% or higher isopropyl rubbing alcohol (drugstore, Walmart)	1/2 cup			Burning Money Demo
9 Volt Battery	1 Cup			Burning Steel Wool Demo
Acetone (Lowes, Home Depot)	1/2 cup			Melting Styrofoam Cup Demo

	Package or		
Active or Fast Rising Yeast	2 Tsp	10 Packages	Elephant Toothpaste Lab
Ammonia	1/4 cup	2 1/2 cups	Acid Attack Lab
Baking Soda	5 Tbsp	3 2/3	Acid Attack Lab, Invisible Ink Activity, Drinkable Acid Demo
Borax (walmart, grocery store, etc)	1/4 tsp	5 tsp	Oobleck Physical Properties
Calcium Chloride (Damprid)	1 Tbsp	1 1/4 cups	Rainbow Flame Lab
Cocoa Powder	1 tsp	1/2 cup	Fake Blood Lab
Coke, 20 oz bottle (save bottle for elephant toothpaste lab)	1	10	Mentos and Diet Coke
Copper Sulfate (Root Killer - Home Depot, Ace Hardware, etc)	1 Tbsp	1 1/4 cups	Rainbow Flame Lab
Corn Starch	2 tsp	1 cup	Fake Blood Lab
Cream of Tartar	1/4 cup	2 1/2 cups	Acid Attack Lab
Dawn Dish Detergent	5 Tbsp	10 Tbsp	Elephant Toothpaste Lab
Diet Coke, 20 oz bottle	1	10	Mentos and Diet Coke
Dollar Bill	1		Burning Money Demo
Fine Steel Wool - Grade 00,000,0000 No Soap	1		Burning Steel Wool Demo
Food Coloring	1	2 boxes	Gas Station Labs, Oobleck Physical Properties, Elephant Toothpaste Lab
Grape or Cranberry Juice Concentrate	1 Tbsp	2/3 cup	Invisible Ink Activity
Hand Sanitizer	4-8 Squirts	4 Bottles	Rainbow Flame Lab
Ice	2-3 cups	20 cups	Melting Ice Lab
Index Card	2	20	Mentos and Diet Coke
Ivory Soap	1 Bar		Exploding Soap Demo
Lemon Juice	1/4 cup	2 1/2 cups	Acid Attack Lab
Lemons	2		Drinkable Acid Demo
Microwave	1		Exploding Soap Demo
Mini Marshmallows	6	30	Gas Station Labs
Powdered Sugar	1 cup	20 cups	Fake Blood Lab
Purple Cabbage	1/4 head	1 head	Acid Attack Lab
Red Food Coloring	25 Drops	2 Tbsp	Fake Blood Lab
Salt	5 Tbsp	3 1/4 cups	Acid Attack Lab, Rainbow Flame Lab. Burning Dollar Demo
Grocery Stores)	1 Tbsp	1 1/4 cups	Rainbow Flame Lab
Sugar	1/4 cup	2 1/2 cups	Demo
Tea Candle	1	3	Gas Station Labs
White Elmer's Glue	2 Tbsp	2 1/2 cups	Oobleck Physical Properties
White Vinegar	1/4 cup	2 1/2 cups	Acid Attack Lab
White, Mint Mentos	10	100	Mentos and Diet Coke

Materials

Materials list grouped by Unit.

Unit	Item	Amount Needed	Partner Amount Same	Amount per Class of 20	Type	Lab
1	Magnifying Glass or Pocket Microscope	1	Group of 4	5	Tool	Mentos and Diet Coke
1	Goggles	1		20	Tool	Mentos and Diet Coke
1	Measuring Tape	1	Group of 4	5	Tool	Mentos and Diet Coke
1	Coke, 20 oz bottle (save bottle for elephant toothpaste lab)	1	Yes	10		Mentos and Diet Coke
1	Diet Coke, 20 oz bottle	1	Yes	10		Mentos and Diet Coke
1	White, Mint Mentos	10	Yes	100		Mentos and Diet Coke
1	Clear Cups	2	Yes	20		Mentos and Diet Coke
1	Index Card	2	Yes	20		Mentos and Diet Coke
2	Clear Cup	1	Yes	10	Tool	Melting Ice Lab
2	Thermometer	1	Yes	10	Tool	Melting Ice Lab
2	Heat Source	1	Yes	10	Tool	Melting Ice Lab
2	Timer (can use phone)	1	Yes	10	Tool	Melting Ice Lab
2	Ice	2-3 cups	Yes	20 cups		Melting Ice Lab
3	2-Liter Bottle, empty	1	Group of 7	3	Dry	Gas Station Labs
3	Balloon	1	Group of 7	3	Dry	Gas Station Labs
3	60 ml Syringe	1	Group of 7	4	Tool	Gas Station Labs
3	Casserole dish or plate with lip	1	Group of 7	3	Tool	Gas Station Labs
3	Mini Marshmallows	6	Group of 7	30		Gas Station Labs
3	Tea Candle	1	Group of 7	3		Gas Station Labs
3	3 drops of food coloring	1	Group of 7	3		Gas Station Labs
4	Ziploc, sandwich or quart	1		20	Dry	Fake Blood Lab
4	Spoon	1		20	Tool	Fake Blood Lab
4	Measuring Teaspoon	1	Group of 4	5	Tool	Fake Blood Lab
4	Powdered Sugar	1 cup		20 cups		Fake Blood Lab
4	Red Food Coloring	25 Drops		2 Tbsp		Fake Blood Lab
4	Cocoa Powder	1 tsp		1/2 cup		Fake Blood Lab
4	Corn Starch	2 tsp		1 cup		Fake Blood Lab
5	Pot holder or Small Towel	1	Yes	10	Dry	Rainbow Flame Lab
5	Disposable Pie or Casserole Tin	1	Yes	10	Tool	Rainbow Flame Lab
5	Goggles	1		20	Tool	Rainbow Flame Lab
5	Long Match or Lighter	1	Groups of 4	5	Tool	Rainbow Flame Lab
5	Table Salt	1 Tbsp	Yes	1.25 Cups		Rainbow Flame Lab
5	Salt Substitute (Potassium Chloride - Grocery Stores)	1 Tbsp	Yes	1.25 Cups		Rainbow Flame Lab

#	Item					
5	Copper Sulfate (Root Killer - Home Depot, Ace Hardware, etc)	1 Tbsp	Yes	1.25 Cups		Rainbow Flame Lab
5	Calcium Chloride (Damprid)	1 Tbsp	Yes	1.25 Cups		Rainbow Flame Lab
5	Hand Sanitizer	4-8 Squirts	Yes	4 Bottles		Rainbow Flame Lab
6	Laminated Periodic Tables or use page protectors instead of laminating.	2 copies		40	Dry	Periodic Table Battleship
6	File or Regular Folder	1		20	Dry	Periodic Table Battleship
6	Tape	2 strips		1-2 rolls	Dry	Periodic Table Battleship
6	Dry Erase Marker	1		20	Dry	Periodic Table Battleship
7	Ziploc, sandwich or quart	1		20	Dry	Oobleck Physical Properties
7	1/4 and 1 Tablespoon	1	Group of 4	5	Tool	Oobleck Physical Properties
7	Cup	1	Group of 2	10		Oobleck Physical Properties
7	Borax (walmart, grocery store, etc)	1/4 tsp		5 tsp		Oobleck Physical Properties
7	White Elmer's Glue	2 Tbsp		2 1/2 cups		Oobleck Physical Properties
7	Food Coloring	4 drops		1 tsp		Oobleck Physical Properties
8	Empty Soda Bottle, empty	1	Yes	10	Dry	Elephant Toothpaste Lab
8	Cup	1	Yes	10	Dry	Elephant Toothpaste Lab
8	Pan or Tray to Catch Mess	1	Yes	10	Tool	Elephant Toothpaste Lab
8	Goggles	1		20	Tool	Elephant Toothpaste Lab
8	40 Volume Hydrogen Peroxide (8-15%) Available at beauty supply stores; Drugstores carry 3% hydrogen peroxide, this will work too but with less effect.	1/2 cup	Yes	5 cups		Elephant Toothpaste Lab
8	Active or Fast Rising Yeast	Package or 2 Tsp	Yes	10 Packages		Elephant Toothpaste Lab
8	Dawn Dish Detergent	1 Tbsp	Yes	10 Tbsp		Elephant Toothpaste Lab
8	Food Coloring	3 drops	Yes	1.5 tsp		Elephant Toothpaste Lab
9	Strainer	1	All	1	Tool	Acid Attack Lab
9	Spoons	2	Group of 4	10	Tool	Acid Attack Lab
9	Purple Cabbage	1/4 head	Group of 5	1 head		Acid Attack Lab
9	Cream of Tartar	1/4 cup	Yes	2 1/2 cups		Acid Attack Lab
9	Baking Soda	1/4 cup	Yes	2 1/2 cups		Acid Attack Lab
9	Ammonia	1/4 cup	Yes	2 1/2 cups		Acid Attack Lab
9	White Vinegar	1/4 cup	Yes	2 1/2 cups		Acid Attack Lab
9	Sugar	1/4 cup	Yes	2 1/2 cups		Acid Attack Lab
9	Salt	1/4 cup	Yes	2 1/2 cups		Acid Attack Lab
9	Lemon Juice	1/4 cup	Yes	2 1/2 cups		Acid Attack Lab
9	Dish Soap	1/4 cup	Yes	2 1/2 cups		Acid Attack Lab
9	Baking Soda	1 Tbsp	Yes	2/3 cup		Invisible Ink Activity
9	Grape or Cranberry Juice Concentrate	1 Tbsp	Yes	2/3 cup		Invisible Ink Activity

Unit	Teacher Demo Items	Amount	Type	Lab
1	Tongs	1	Tool	Burning Money
1	Lighter or Match	1	Tool	Burning Money
1	Dollar Bill	1		Burning Money
1	70% or higher isopropyl rubbing alcohol (drugstore, Walmart)	1/2 cup		Burning Money
1	Salt	1/4 tsp		Burning Money
3	Ivory Soap	1 Bar		Exploding Soap
3	Microwave	1		Exploding Soap
7	Glass dish or disposable pie pan	1	Tool	Melting Styrofoam Cup
7	Styrofoam Cup	1		Melting Styrofoam Cup
7	Acetone (Lowes, Home Depot)	1/2 cup		Melting Styrofoam Cup
8	No Soap	1	Tool	Burning Steel Wool
8	9 Volt Battery	1 Cup		Burning Steel Wool
9	Lemons	2		Drinkable Acid
9	Sugar	1 tsp		Drinkable Acid
9	Baking Soda	1/2 tsp		Drinkable Acid

Made in the USA
Columbia, SC
15 August 2020